Tourism Today

Editor: Tracy Biram

Volume 365

Independence Educational Publishers

First published by Independence Educational Publishers

The Studio, High Green

Great Shelford

Cambridge CB22 5EG

England

ISBN-13: 978 1 86168 822 4

Printed in Great Britain

Zenith Print Group

Contents

Introduction

Tourism Today is Volume 365 in the **ISSUES** series. The aim of the series is to offer current, diverse information about important issues in our world, from a UK perspective.

ABOUT TOURISM TODAY

Tourism supports one in 10 jobs across the world, so the impact that tourists can have is massive. People are travelling further than ever before, but what effect does this have on the people and environments that are visited? This book explores the benefits and disadvantages of tourism and looks at how we can all become responsible tourists.

OUR SOURCES

Titles in the **ISSUES** series are designed to function as educational resource books, providing a balanced overview of a specific subject.

The information in our books is comprised of facts, articles and opinions from many different sources, including:

◆ Newspaper reports and opinion pieces

◆ Website factsheets

◆ Magazine and journal articles

◆ Statistics and surveys

◆ Government reports

◆ Literature from special interest groups.

A NOTE ON CRITICAL EVALUATION

Because the information reprinted here is from a number of different sources, readers should bear in mind the origin of the text and whether the source is likely to have a particular bias when presenting information (or when conducting their research). It is hoped that, as you read about the many aspects of the issues explored in this book, you will critically evaluate the information presented.

It is important that you decide whether you are being presented with facts or opinions. Does the writer give a biased or unbiased report? If an opinion is being expressed, do you agree with the writer? Is there potential bias to the 'facts' or statistics behind an article?

ASSIGNMENTS

In the back of this book, you will find a selection of assignments designed to help you engage with the articles you have been reading and to explore your own opinions. Some tasks will take longer than others and there is a mixture of design, writing and research-based activities that you can complete alone or in a group.

FURTHER RESEARCH

At the end of each article we have listed its source and a website that you can visit if you would like to conduct your own research. Please remember to critically evaluate any sources that you consult and consider whether the information you are viewing is accurate and unbiased.

Useful Websites

www.blacks.co.uk/blog

www.cardiff.ac.uk

www.cocobutterblog.co.uk

www.frontier.ac.uk

www.independent.co.uk

www.ons.gov.uk

www.politico.eu

www.sumas.ch

www.sustainability-times.com

www.telegraph.co.uk

www.theconversation.com

www.theecologist.org

www.theguardian.com

www.weforum.org

www.worldatlas.com

www.yougov.co.uk

What is travel and tourism?

Travel

There are many reasons why people travel, but generally they are split into three categories:

◆ Leisure Travel – includes travel for holidays, cultural events, recreation or sports.

◆ Business Travel – includes meetings, conferences and exhibitions; usually business travellers have their expenses paid by their company.

◆ Visiting friends and relatives (VFR) – includes all travel for the purpose of meeting friends and relatives, either within your own country or abroad.

Types of tourism

Domestic tourism – taking holidays and trips in your own country.

• An example would be a family from Leeds taking a short break to the seaside resort of Brighton.

International tourism – visiting a different country than the one that you live in. It can be broken into two categories:

◆ Inbound tourism – visitors from overseas coming into the country.

• For example, a tourist coming from Germany to the UK.

◆ Outbound tourism – travelling to a different country. Generally, when we use the term outbound tourism in the UK we are referring to UK residents travelling out of the UK.

• For example, you are an outbound tourist from the UK if you go to France on holiday.

Tourism categories

Some of the different types of tourism are:

Adventure tourism – involves travelling to take part in physically challenging outdoor activities such as mountain climbing, hiking or kayaking.

Cultural tourism – involves travel that visits cultural or historical places and events.

Ecotourism or sustainable tourism – is responsible travel to areas that support local communities and help preserve the environment.

Dark tourism – travelling to places associated with death and suffering.

Religious tourism – travelling for the purpose of pilgrimage or visiting religious sites.

Rural tourism – similar to ecotourism, rural tourism includes travel to rural destinations, such as farm stays or walking holidays.

Voluntourism – travellers participate in voluntary work, often with the emphasis on helping people rather than the environment.

Wellness tourism – travelling for health and well-being reasons.

Of course, there are many more types of tourism, and some travellers fall into multiple categories.

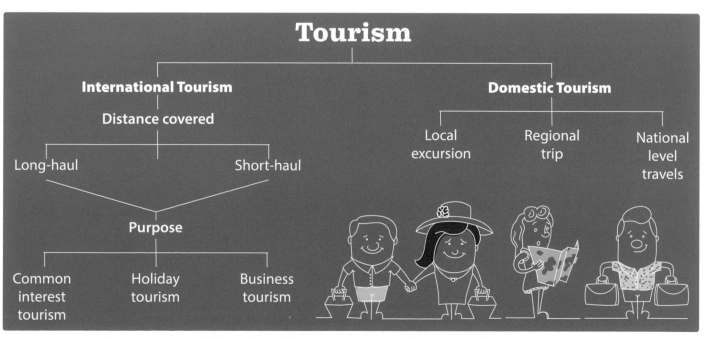

Tourism

International Tourism	Domestic Tourism

Distance covered

Local excursion   Regional trip   National level travels

Long-haul   Short-haul

Purpose

Common interest tourism   Holiday tourism   Business tourism

Travel trends: 2018

Annual estimates of travel and tourism visits to the UK (of less than 12 months' duration) and associated earnings and expenditure between the UK and the rest of the world.

◆ There were fewer overseas residents' visits to the UK in 2018 than in 2017 and also a fall in the number of visits abroad by UK residents.

◆ A total of 37.9 million visits were made by overseas residents to the UK in 2018, which was 3% fewer than in 2017.

◆ There were 71.7 million visits overseas by UK residents in 2018, a decrease of 1% when compared with 2017.

◆ UK residents spent £45.4 billion on visits overseas in 2018, which was 1% more than in 2017.

◆ Overseas residents spent £22.9 billion on visits to the UK in 2018, a decrease of 7% compared with 2017.

◆ The most frequent reason for visits was for holidays, both for UK residents visiting abroad and overseas residents visiting the UK.

Both UK trips abroad and visits to the UK have decreased in 2018

There were 71.7 million visits overseas by UK residents in 2018, a decrease of 1% compared with 2017.

Overall, visits have increased over the last 20 years, although notable falls were observed in 2009 and 2010. Since then, numbers have increased again and, in each of the years from 2016 to 2018, UK visits abroad have exceeded the numbers seen in 2008 (before the decrease).

There were 37.9 million visits by overseas residents to the UK in 2018, 3% less than in 2017. This is the first time overseas visits have fallen since 2010.

Visits to the UK by overseas residents and visits overseas by UK residents both fell in 2018 compared with 2017

Visits to and from the UK, 1998 to 2018

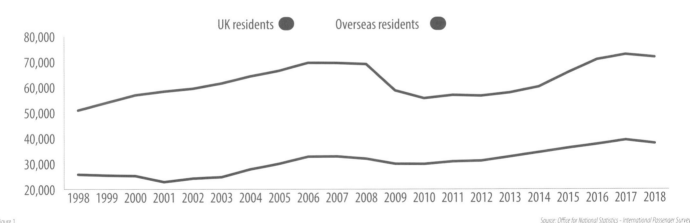

Figure 1

Spending on visits to the UK fell by 7% in 2018, but spending abroad by UK residents increased by 1%

Spending on visits to and from the UK, 1998 to 2018

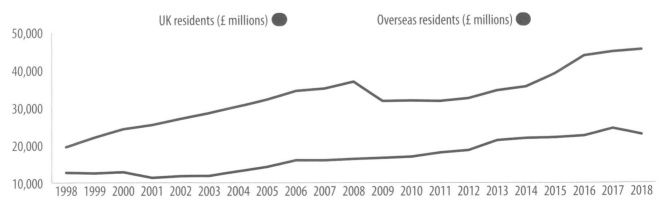

Figure 2

UK residents spent £45.4 billion on visits abroad in 2018, which was 1% more than in 2017. Although UK residents spent more money abroad in 2018, this is a much smaller increase than in previous years. UK residents also spent fewer nights away when compared with 2017 and this may be one reason for the smaller increase.

Overseas residents spent £22.9 billion on visits to the UK in 2018, a decrease of 7% compared with 2017 (Figure 2). The decrease in spending was larger than the decrease in the number of visits (3%). One possible factor in the larger fall in spending is average length of visit, which decreased from 7.3 nights in 2017 to 7.0 nights in 2018.

Holidays are still the most common reason for visiting the UK

The fall in visits to the UK was seen across all types of trips (Figure 3). There were 15.1 million holiday visits to the UK in 2018, a decrease of 2% when compared with 2017 (15.4 million). However, the number of holiday visits in 2017 was the highest recorded and the 2018 figure is in keeping with the general trend observed in recent years. Holiday visits remained the most common reason for visiting the UK and accounted for 40% of the total.

◆ Visits to friends and family fell for the first time since 2013 (by 2% to 11.8 million).

◆ Miscellaneous visits decreased by 16% to 2.6 million.

◆ Business trips fell from 8.8 million in 2017 to 8.4 million in 2018, a decrease of 4%.

Holidays were the most frequent reason for visiting the UK between 1998 and 2018

Overseas residents visits to the UK by purpose, 1998 to 2018

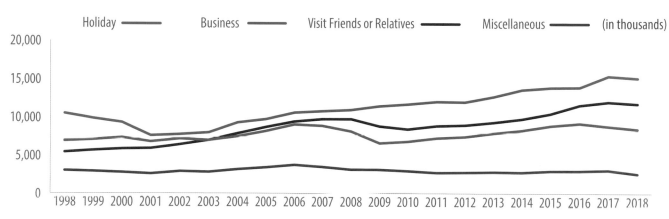

Figure 3

Source: Office for National Statistics - International Passenger Survey

There were 3.9 million visits to the UK by residents of the USA in 2018, more than any other country. This was the same as the number of visits in 2017 although US residents were then the second-most frequent visitors to the UK. This is because visits by French residents fell from 4.0 million in 2017 to 3.7 million in 2018. In 2018, French residents were the second-most likely to visit the UK.

Of the 10 countries whose residents visited the UK the most frequently in 2018, eight were EU countries (Figure 4). The non-EU countries were the USA and Australia (1.0 million visits, the 10th-highest total). The top 10 list was unchanged from 2017, apart from France and the USA swapping between first and second place. The list of top 10 countries whose residents visit the UK has remained largely stable over recent years.

Residents of the USA visited the UK most in 2018, ahead of France and Germany

Top 10 visiting countries: number of visits, 2018

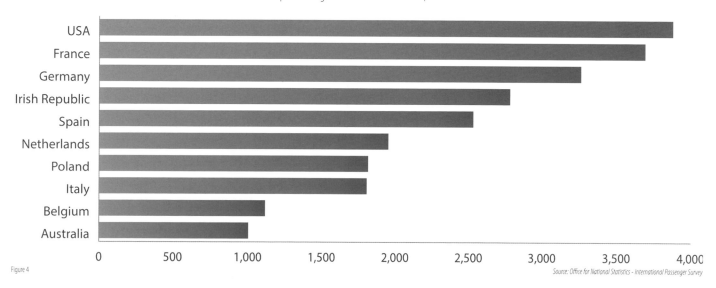

Figure 4

Source: Office for National Statistics - International Passenger Survey

Outside London, the towns most visited from overseas in 2018 were Edinburgh, Manchester, Birmingham and Glasgow

Top 20 UK towns visited for at least one night, 2018 (excluding London)

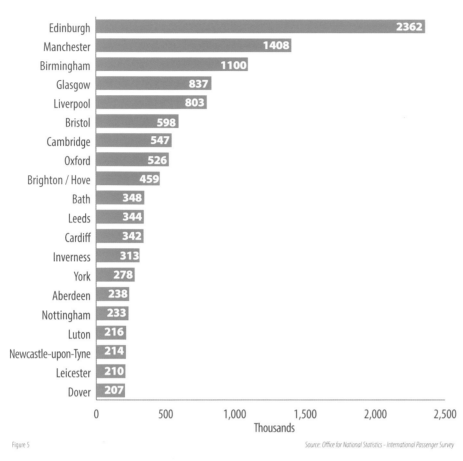

Town	Thousands
Edinburgh	2362
Manchester	1408
Birmingham	1100
Glasgow	837
Liverpool	803
Bristol	598
Cambridge	547
Oxford	526
Brighton / Hove	459
Bath	348
Leeds	344
Cardiff	342
Inverness	313
York	278
Aberdeen	238
Nottingham	233
Luton	216
Newcastle-upon-Tyne	214
Leicester	210
Dover	207

Figure 5

Source: Office for National Statistics – International Passenger Survey

London, Edinburgh, Manchester and Birmingham each attracted over 1 million stays from overseas visitors

London attracted 19.1 million overnight visits in 2018, far more than any other town or city. More than half of visits to the UK included a trip to London.

Overnight visits to cities other than London are shown in Figure 5. Edinburgh (2.4 million), Manchester (1.4 million) and Birmingham (1.1 million) each received more than 1 million overnight visits.

UK residents' visits abroad decreased in 2018, to the second-highest total recorded

There were 71.7 million visits overseas by UK residents in 2018, the second-highest figure recorded by the International Passenger Survey (IPS). The number of visits in 2018 was 1% fewer than in 2017, when there were 72.8 million visits.

The most common reason for travelling abroad was for holidays. There were 47.0 million holiday visits abroad by UK residents, 1% more than in 2017 and accounting for almost two-thirds (66%) of visits. By comparison, there were 32.3 million holiday visits abroad 20 years earlier, in 1998 (Figure 6).

There were 16.7 million visits overseas to visit friends and family in 2018 (5% fewer than in 2017) and 6.6 million business visits (3% fewer than in 2017). The fall in business visits abroad by UK residents mirrors the fall in business visits to the UK made by overseas residents.

Holidays were easily the most frequent reason for visits abroad between 1998 and 2018

UK residents' visits abroad by purpose, 1998 to 2018

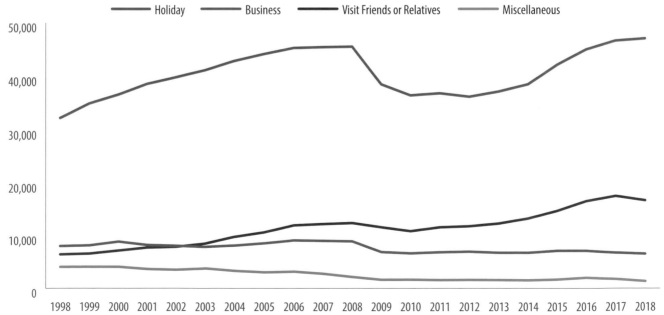

Legend: Holiday — Business — Visit Friends or Relatives — Miscellaneous

Figure 6

Source: Office for National Statistics – International Passenger Survey

UK residents visited Spain the most in 2018, followed by France, Italy and the USA

Top 10 countries visited by UK residents, 2018

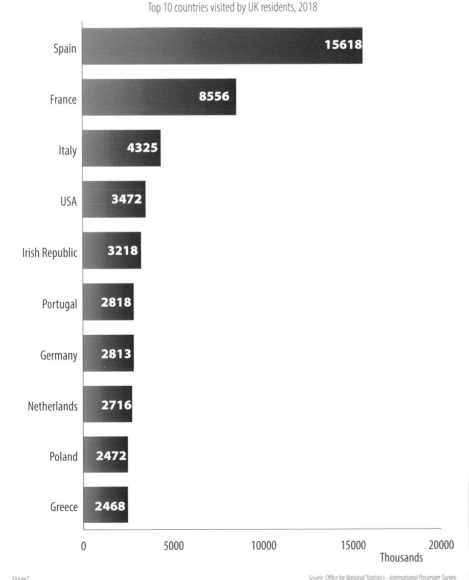

Country	Thousands
Spain	15618
France	8556
Italy	4325
USA	3472
Irish Republic	3218
Portugal	2818
Germany	2813
Netherlands	2716
Poland	2472
Greece	2468

Figure7

Source: Office for National Statistics - International Passenger Survey

Spain is still the most visited country by UK residents

There were 15.6 million visits to Spain by UK residents in 2018, a decrease of 2% from 2017 and the first time this number has fallen since 2009. Visits to Spain were mainly for holidays (89% of the total).

Spain, France, Italy, the USA and the Republic of Ireland, in that order, remain the top five most popular countries for UK residents to visit (Figure 7), accounting for 49% of all visits abroad and approximately 41% of total spend abroad. Overall, 75% of visits were to EU countries, the same as in 2017.

Among the top 10 most visited countries, Poland saw the biggest percentage change between 2017 and 2018, decreasing by 7% from 2.7 million to 2.5 million, of these, 66% were to visit friends and family. Other changes included increases in visits to Turkey (up from 1.2 million in 2017 to 1.4 million in 2018) and in visits to Tunisia (although the numbers remain small, at 170,000). There was a decrease in visits to Australia of 21%, from 450,000 to 360,000.

24 May 2019

Global tourism hits record highs – but who goes where on holiday?

As the holiday season approaches, we look at the rise and rise of tourism and find out where the world's 1.4 billion international travellers go on vacation.

By Molly Blackall

How many people travel abroad on holiday?

Tourism is on the rise. In 2018, there were a record 1.4 billion international tourist arrivals, according to the World Tourism Organization (UNWTO), a rise of 6% over 2017. That doesn't mean 1.4 billion people travel abroad for their holidays, as many people will clock up more than one trip.

But it does mean tourism is playing an increasingly important role in the global economy. In 2018, it was worth about $1.7 trillion (£1.3 trillion), or about 2% of total global GDP. Even the UNWTO is struggling to keep up, with current figures vastly exceeding expectations.

In 1950 there were 25 million international tourist visits, rising to 166 million in 1970, and 435 million in 1990.

The growth of budget airlines has made travelling more accessible, with passengers able to fly from London Stansted to Düsseldorf for just £7.99. For many Londoners, this costs less than a day's commute.

Nikodem Szumilo, associate professor of economics and finance of the built environment at UCL, says the growth of the global tourist industry is partly due to the rise of digital services. 'The most recent development in the industry was a small revolution of online reviews and online bookings which reduced prices but increased satisfaction,' he says. 'This means that more people travel more often.'

What are the most popular destinations?

According to the UNWTO, four-fifths of tourists travel within their own region. Continuing a long-term trend, Europe leads the way in overseas visits, receiving 713 million visitors last year alone.

Globally, France leads the way, followed by Spain, the US, China and Italy. The UK is the seventh-most visited country in the world.

However, other regions are on the rise. Last year, trips to North Africa rose 10%, and tourism to sub-Saharan Africa and the Middle East is also increasing, as demand for unconventional destinations grows.

In 2018, Uber ranked the most visited destinations around the world for its users. The Empire State Building in New York claimed first place, followed by the city's Freedom Tower and CN Tower in Toronto. The Arc de Triomphe and Eiffel Tower in Paris completed the top five.

Buckingham Palace, the only British attraction in the top 15, came seventh ahead of the Berlin Wall, the Vatican, Disneyland and the Egyptian pyramids.

So which country provides the most visitors?

The number of tourists produced by a country tends to correlate with its income and population.

China's rising wealth has resulted in a huge growth of tourism abroad, making Chinese people the world's most abundant tourists. In 2017, Chinese tourists made 143 million journeys abroad, followed by Germany (92 million), the US (87.8 million) and the UK (74.2 million).

According to the Office for National Statistics, UK residents consistently make more visits abroad than foreign residents make to Britain. Favoured destinations are Spain, France and Italy. Three in four Britons remain within the EU, but the US was the fourth-most visited location for UK citizens last year.

Tourism is growing rapidly in Russia, whose tourist numbers rose by 16% last year. France and Australia are increasingly important players, increasing by 10% and 9%, respectively.

Who comes to the UK?

Unsurprisingly, London was the UK's most popular destination, with more than half of all UK visits including a trip to the capital. Edinburgh was the second hottest tourist spot, and Manchester third.

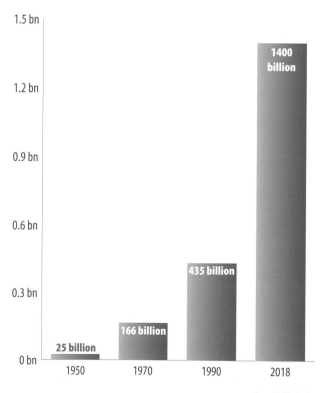

Global tourism has increased exponentially since the end of the second world war

- 25 billion (1950)
- 166 billion (1970)
- 435 billion (1990)
- 1400 billion (2018)

Source: World Tourism Organization

Americans top the list of arrivals, but four-fifths of the UK's most-visiting countries were from Europe.

How important is tourism to the UK?

The tourist industry is responsible for about 2.5% of British GDP. Last year, visitors spent almost £23 billion in the UK, though visitor numbers fell slightly on 2017 (a record year).

In spite of this dip, Visit Britain – the official tourism board – estimates that by 2025 Britain's tourism industry could be worth as much as 10% of GDP and will employ more than one in 10 people.

Will Brexit have an impact?

Claudio Milano from Ostelea School of Tourism doesn't think so, calling the supposed link between Brexit and tourism 'mainly political propaganda'.

He said that the most likely impact of Brexit on the tourist industry is on labour patterns. 'Tourism is a sector which is based on migrant workers,' he says. 'So Brexit will have more of impact on tourism's workforce than on the attractiveness of the UK.'

A brief history of tourism

Tourism may seem like a modern notion, dominated by no-frills air flights, selfie sticks and Lonely Planet guides. In reality, touristic tendencies began long before the birth of EasyJet and Airbnb.

Archeological digs have shown that early civilisations such as the Phoenicians, Mayans and the Shang dynasty all travelled in pursuit of curiosity as well as commerce.

The origins of tourism may also lie in religion. Early pilgrimages, such as those to Mecca and Buddhist sites, provide some of the earliest examples of humans travelling to visit popular destinations.

Paul Stock, associate professor of international history at the London School of Economics, traces the foundations of modern tourism to 'the Grand Tour', a travelling trend in the 17th century. At this time, aristocrats began travelling a particular route around Europe – beginning in Paris, moving to southern France, visiting Italy, and travelling back to England via Germany. Early reports show that many tourist activities of the Grand Tour are similar to today, with examples of souvenir collecting, drunkenness and partying, and even sex tourism.

Travellers often began the tour after finishing their studies, a sort of Enlightenment gap year. Perhaps today's generation of backpackers aren't so original after all.

Paul Stock certainly thinks so. 'Virtually every aspect of modern holiday-going, with the single exception of sunbathing, can be traced back to the period of the Grand Tour,' he said in an educational film on the topic.

It's hard to determine when these patterns evolved into a clear industry, but Thomas Cook, founder of the popular travel company, began his first excursion in 1841. He is widely considered the 'father of modern tourism'.

Sun, culture, jobs, growth – what's not to like?

Er… overcrowding, rising property prices, planeloads of stag parties marauding through Euro capitals with penis-tiaras on their heads: there is a dark side to tourism.

Hotspots around the world are struggling under the weight of 'over-tourism', which threatens massive destruction of local environments and communities.

Tourists are responsible for large quantities of single-use plastics that pollute beaches and threaten wildlife, and souvenir hunters have been known to break off pieces of endangered coral to keep as memorabilia.

While traffic and overcrowding are well documented side effects of tourism, Szumilo says intense pressure on hospitals and public transport from tourists can also strain resources, leaving public services unable to cater for locals.

Szumilo highlights the impact of holiday homes on local communities. Often empty for most of the year, second homes can reduce supply for locals, limit economic growth and raise house prices.

'When we talk about travel and tourism, we think about beaches, holiday resorts, and iconic sceneries,' says Marina Novelli, professor of tourism and international development at the University of Brighton.

'We tend not to think about space politics, social justice, gender equality, poverty alleviation, environmental management or the impact that epidemics or conflicts may inflict on destinations.'

What's to blame?

According to Milano, the phenomenon of over-tourism comes partially from the rise in global mobility. Increased transnational travel has led to rising numbers of international students, migrant workers, second home residents, and even journalists working overseas. He also emphasises the role of neoliberalism, which he says is turning cities from 'locations to destinations'.

The rise of short-term letting apps has also been blamed. Last month, 10 European cities issued a joint letter to the EU demanding help in their battle against Airbnb. The company has long been criticised for its role in housing shortages, raising house prices and displacing local residents.

What are countries doing about it?

Last month, the picturesque city of Bruges announced it would stop advertising day trips, limit the number of cruise ships docking nearby and shift docking times to ease the weekend rush.

The UNESCO world heritage site has experienced a 28% rise in tourism in the past two years, with the mayor, Dirk De Fauw, doubting the city's ability to cope with mounting numbers of tourists. 'We have to control the influx more if we don't want Bruges to become a complete Disneyland here,' he says.

Last year another UNESCO world heritage site, Dubrovnik, announced limitations on cruise ships. After overcrowding in ancient alleyways, outdoor tables were also restricted, and new crackdowns were imposed on street vendors catering to swathes of tourists.

Following in the footsteps of popular Majorca, Rome – which hosts 15.2 million tourists annually – recently announced restrictions on antisocial tourist behaviour. The measures include a crackdown on drunk and disorderly conduct and a ban on shirtless sightseeing.

After causing structural damage to picturesque bridges around the world, love padlocks – attached by romantic partners – are also coming under new regulation.

Bridges in Paris have already begun their removal, with the deputy mayor saying 'they spoil the aesthetics of the bridge, are structurally bad for it and can cause accidents'.

Hardly the best omen for relationships, but perhaps the only way to save the City of Love.

However, these targeted measures may not be enough. Milano says that to meaningfully change the tourist industry, we first need to change the way we understand it.

'Tourism is generally only measured in the number of international arrivals, but we need new indicators and a new set of measures of tourism,' he says. 'For example, do we have gender equality in our tourist industries? Why are men always executives? Are jobs in tourism decent? What about the liveability of local residents? It's a question at a political level about how we define and understand tourism.'

1 July 2019

The history of Thomas Cook, from tours for teetotallers to boozy packages in Spain

Thomas Cook, one of Britain's oldest travel companies, ceased trading last night. Here, Chris Leadbeater recalls a trip down memory lane with the company's archivist.

Thomas Cook. The two words have become synonymous with the modern concept of package travel, but they come with plenty of heritage. The company can trace its origins back 178 years, when the very first tour was organised by a Leicestershire printer who could not have envisaged that his simple scheme would become a colossal company.

Born in the Derbyshire market town of Melbourne in 1808, Thomas Cook was a man of religious conviction who, in 1841, began dabbling in transport plans for his fellow followers of the temperance (abstinence from alcohol) movement. That first jaunt was a rail hop from Leicester to Loughborough – but operations quickly expanded beyond local trains. A tour to Liverpool, just four years on, was booked by 1,200 people. It was so popular that Cook had to repeat it, for 800 further customers, a fortnight later.

The brand has survived two world wars, the reigns of six British monarchs, the rise and fall of the Soviet bloc and numerous changes to how we live. Not least the invention of flight.

'The company has witnessed a good deal,' says Paul Smith, the company's archivist, picking up a brochure which marks one of the moments when British tourists became airborne. 'Thomas Cook was the first travel agent to market pleasure flights,' he adds. 'We placed an advert in *The Times* in Easter 1919. And we produced this.' It is, in truth, an unremarkable testament to so seismic a time – a pamphlet in drab olive-brown, a photograph of a converted First World War Handley Page bomber as a sole cover photograph. But the dream it is selling is there in the few metres of space between the plane's wheels and the ground, a new era dawned.

There are plenty of other such echoes of a changing planet in Paul's boxes and files. A 1928 brochure sings of the good days just before the Wall Street Crash, touting a tie-in between Thomas Cook and Cunard which started and ended in New York. It journeyed through the Caribbean and down the flank of South America to Buenos Aires, headed across the Atlantic to Cape Town, turned north along the torso of Africa in search of Cairo – then returned to the Big Apple via Naples, Monte Carlo and Madeira. The price for this princely expedition is listed as US$5,000 – around £50,000 today, Paul estimates.

Other artefacts retreat into the 19th century. The brochure that the firm produced in 1868 – the second time such literature was published after an initial experiment in 1865 proved successful – is a thing of joy, more geography textbook than promotional spiel. It is filled with maps which chart available travel routes, red lines spider-webbing across Europe to Rouen and Paris, Bologna and Florence. A reproduction of a Thomas Cook 'circular note' – an in-house version of the traveller's cheque – recalls a move into currency transactions in 1874. A *Nile Season: 1896-97* brochure salutes the rise of river cruising.

Further items shed breezy light onto the 20th century – a Fifties belle adorning a pamphlet for the company's Prestatyn holiday camp that shouts: 'This Is It! Your 1954 Holiday'; a 1963 brochure, disguised as a women's magazine called *Holidaymaking*, firmly aimed at female decision-makers in evolving households; big hair and palm trees for gaudy 1985, youthful romance on a Greek island for 1996. Others deal in shadows – instructions on how to use the 'Enemy Mail Service' that Thomas Cook helped to run in the Second World War, deploying company connections to deliver letters to people in occupied lands.

The company has, of course, also changed after nearly two centuries. The Cook family sold it in 1928, and it has seen subsequent periods of national as well as private ownership. 'But we've been trading under the same name throughout,'

Paul adds. 'Those two words "Thomas Cook" have been there since Day One.' He of all people would know.

A brief history of Thomas Cook

1841: Thomas Cook started organising leisure trips in the summer of 1841 when its founder, who gave his name to the company, organised a successful one-day rail excursion at a shilling a head from Leicester to Loughborough. During the next three summers Mr Cook arranged a succession of trips, taking passengers to Leicester, Nottingham, Derby and Birmingham. Four years later, he organised his first trip abroad, taking a group from Leicester to Calais. This was followed in the 1860s by trips to Switzerland, Italy, Egypt and America.

1865: In partnership with his son, John Mason Cook, he opened an office in Fleet Street in 1865. In accordance with his beliefs, Mr Cook senior and his wife also ran a small temperance hotel above the office. The firm's growing importance was demonstrated in 1884, when it transported a relief force to rescue General Gordon, from Khartoum, in Sudan.

1869: In 1869, he hired two steamers and conducted his first party up the Nile. The climax of his career, however, came in September 1872 when, at the age of 63, he departed from Leicester on a tour of the world that would keep him away from home for almost eight months. It had long been his ambition to travel 'to Egypt via China', but such a trip only became practicable at the end of 1869 following the opening of the Suez Canal and the completion of a rail network linking the east and west coasts of America.

1924: The company was incorporated as Thos Cook & Son Ltd in 1924, and in 1926 the headquarters moved from Ludgate Circus to Berkeley Street, Mayfair, a once aristocratic area which was now the centre of London society. Then, in 1928, Thomas Cook's surviving grandsons, Frank and Ernest, unexpectedly sold the business to the Belgian Compagnie Internationale des Wagons-Lits et des Grands Express Européens, operators of most of Europe's luxury sleeping cars, including the Orient Express.

1945: Thomas Cook was nationalised shortly after the Second World War when it became part of the state-owned British Railways. It benefited from a holiday boom after the conflict, which saw one million Britons travelling abroad by 1950.

1965: In 1965, Thomas Cook's profits exceeded £1 million for the first time, but it was facing stiff competition from younger rivals.

1977: It was privatised in the 1970s with Midland Bank becoming its sole owner in 1977. Thomas Cook managed to survive the recession of the 1970s – a recession that witnessed the collapse of several travel firms – and enhanced its reputation for providing excellent service by launching a Money Back Guarantee scheme in 1974. It was sold by Midland in 1992 to a German bank and charter airline.

2001: C&N Touristic AG, one of Germany's largest travel groups, became the sole owner of Thomas Cook in 2001 and a new chapter in the company's history began. Within a matter of months, C&N Touristic AG had changed its name to Thomas Cook AG and launched a new logo and brand identity. In the UK, Thomas Cook introduced its new three-tier mass-market brand strategy – Thomas Cook, JMC and Sunset – and the newly-branded Thomas Cook Airlines was launched in March 2003.

2019: Thomas Cook, one of the world's biggest leisure travel groups, with sales of £7.8 billion, 19 million annual customers and 22,000 employees, ceased trading in September 2019.

23 September 2019

Holidays in the 1990s and now

Since the 1990s, we're going on more holidays... but they're shorter than they used to be. Explore three decades of changing tourism habits.

In the last 20 years, UK tourists have turned their backs on traditional 2-week holidays in favour of short breaks and week-long trips. And one-day 'booze cruises' across the Channel to stock up on alcohol and cigarettes are much less common than they used to be.

Going abroad on holiday in the 1990s was very different. Hardly anyone had access to the internet, so you probably booked your trip by going to a travel agent or finding a cheap package deal on Teletext. Once you arrived at your destination, clutching your guide book, film camera and travellers cheques, you were pretty incommunicado, unless you found a phone box or an internet cafe.

We looked at data from our International Passenger Survey in 1996 and 2016 to uncover the biggest differences in our holiday habits between the 1990s and now.

We're going on more holidays...

In 2016, UK residents went on more than 45 million foreign holidays, up from 27 million in 1996. That's a 68% rise in the number of holidays, while the UK population increased by 12% in the same period.

...but they're shorter than they used to be

One of the biggest changes we've seen over the last 20 years is the marked decline in the popularity of 2-week holidays and the rise of short breaks.

The week-long break is a lot more popular than before, and there's also been an increase in the number of holidays lasting 10 nights.

UK residents are making far fewer day-trips abroad than they did 20 years ago. This could be because many of these visits were 'booze cruises' – journeys across the English Channel to stock up on alcohol and cigarettes – which are no longer as cost-efficient as they used to be. Duty-free sales within the EU ended in 1999, France has been ratcheting up the price of cigarettes since 2000, and in recent years the pound has fallen in value against the euro.

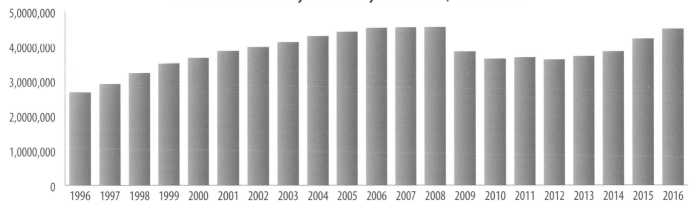

Total number of holidays overseas by UK residents, 1996 to 2016

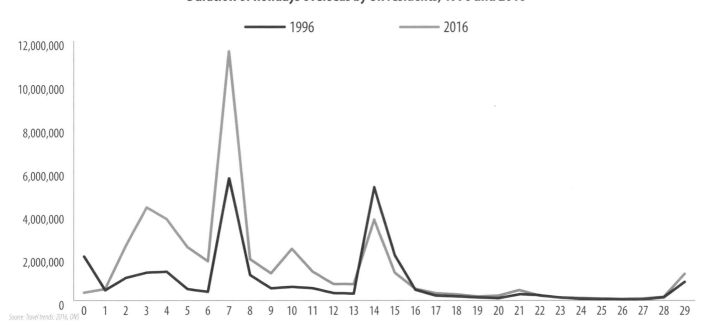

Duration of holidays overseas by UK residents, 1996 and 2016

—— 1996 —— 2016

Source: Travel trends: 2016, ONS

Top 10 destinations for UK resident holidaymakers, 2016 (with 1996 figures)

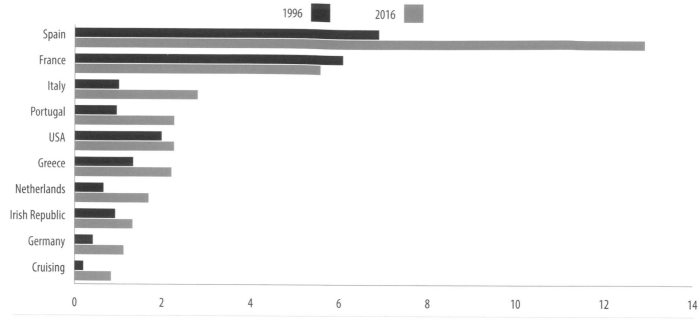

Number of holidays by UK residents, selected countries, 1996 and 2016

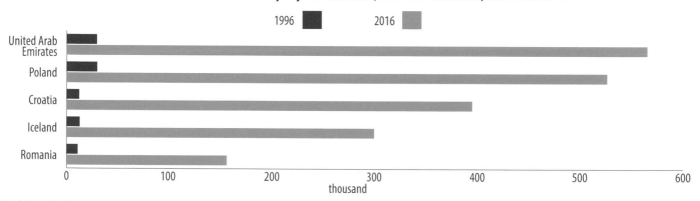

thousand

Source: Travel trends: 2016, ONS

No-frills airlines have taken off

One of the most likely explanations for UK residents going on more, shorter, holidays is the growth of the budget airlines.

Throughout the 1980s and 1990s, the European Council relaxed the rules to create a common aviation area across Europe, allowing low-cost carriers including easyJet and Ryanair to enter the market.

Between 1996 and 2015 (the most recent figures available from the Civil Aviation Authority), passenger numbers at UK airports increased by 85%, from 135 million to 251 million – continuing a long-term trend. And according to the UN's International Civil Aviation Organisation in 2003, 'around 50% of the traffic on low-cost carriers is newly generated' – which means half of the people flying on budget airlines in Europe weren't making those journeys before.

Top 10 destinations for UK holidaymakers

Comparing the most popular holiday destinations in 1996 and 2016, not a lot has changed at the top of the chart: we still love visiting Spain and France.

However, while the number of holidays to Spain has rocketed (up 87% in 20 years), France is one of the few countries we're visiting less than we were in 1996: the number of holidays by UK residents has fallen by 9%.

Budget airlines may be behind this too: rather than driving to France on a ferry (the number of holidaymakers travelling by sea has declined by 33% since 1996), tourists are perhaps opting for a cheap flight elsewhere instead.

Germany has now joined the top 10 destinations for UK holidaymakers, and another new entry is cruising – which is now four times as popular as it was 20 years ago. This could be due to an ageing population, with increasing numbers of older people in the population – but cruise operators are also trying to extend their appeal to younger holidaymakers too.

Two destinations that have dropped out of the top 10 since 1996 are Belgium and Turkey.

Outside the top 10

Further down the rankings, we can look at some countries that have become a lot more popular with UK resident holidaymakers since 1996.

The United Arab Emirates' (UAE's) popularity with British holidaymakers is especially striking. It's largely due to the popularity of Dubai, where the UAE has invested heavily

Number of holidays by UK residents, selected countries, 1996 and 2016

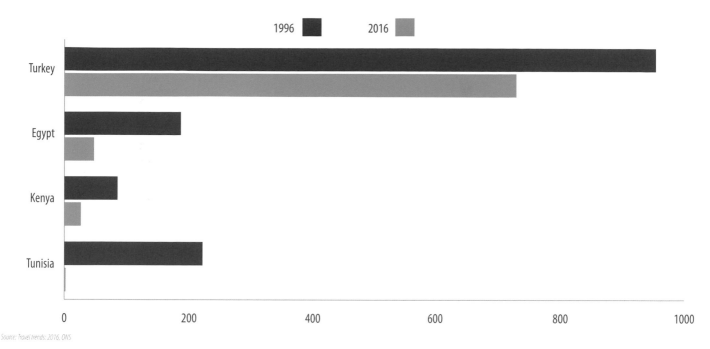

1996 ■   2016 ▨

Turkey
Egypt
Kenya
Tunisia

0   200   400   600   800   1000

Source: Travel trends: 2016, ONS

in hotels and shopping malls, and has been rewarded with ever-greater numbers of British tourists.

Poland and Romania have joined the EU in the intervening years (in 2004 and 2007, respectively), and Romanian nationals gained full rights to work in the UK in 2014. This made travel between the countries much simpler. In 2016 many of the UK resident holidaymakers were nationals of the countries they visited (69% of those visiting Romania for holidays were Romanian and 31% of those going to Poland were Polish), perhaps returning to spend the holidays with family and friends.

Croatia joined the EU in 2013, and the dramatic rise in visitor numbers partially reflects the emergence of the country from the Balkans War, which only ended in late 1995.

Iceland's newfound popularity is less straightforward to explain – the rise in the numbers of UK holidaymakers began around 2010, just two years after the economic crisis devalued the Icelandic krona, making the country much more affordable for foreign tourists.

2010 was also the year that the volcano Eyjafjallajokull erupted, sending clouds of ash into the skies above Europe and grounding planes across the world, and some think that the TV pictures of Iceland shown around the globe encouraged visitors to go there. 'Secret to Iceland's Tourism Boom? A Financial Crash and a Volcanic Eruption' read the headline in *The New York Times*.

Only five countries with significant visitor numbers suffered a decline in the numbers of holidaymakers. Besides France (see 'Top 10 destinations for UK holidaymakers' section), the countries that saw the biggest falls were those that have experienced terrorist incidents and security concerns in recent years: Turkey, Egypt, Kenya and Tunisia.

7 August 2017

WHERE IS EVERYONE?

www.ons.gov.uk

Britons make worst tourists, say Britons (and Spaniards and Germans)

We are the country with the most negative view of its own tourists.

By Matthew Smith

An international YouGov study shows that tales of British rowdiness overseas are now part of the popular consciousness; Britons are the most likely among 26 countries to take a negative view of their own tourists.

More than half of us (57%) hold an unfavourable opinion of British tourists, and just 29% take a positive view.

We are, in fact, the only country that feels so much more negatively about our own tourists; the next comparable country is Germany where the 43% who think Germans behave badly on holiday is largely matched by the 40% who think their brethren give their country a good name.

These figures are a far cry from those from the Philippines, where a whopping 85% hold a favourable view of Filipinos vacationing abroad and only 11% feel the opposite way.

Unsurprisingly, Britons are also the most likely to think that the locals in foreign resorts also take a dim view of our holidaymakers. More than six in ten (61%) think that residents have a negative opinion of British tourists, and only 23% believe that we are gladly received by natives.

Britain is the country with the most negative view of its own tourists

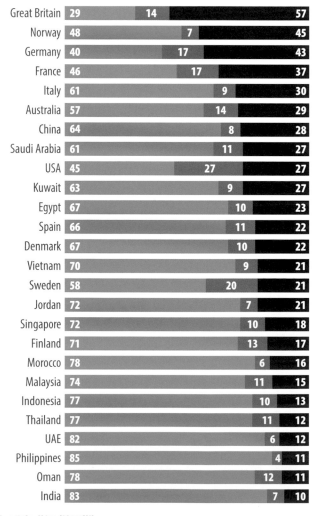

Positive ● **Don't know** ● **Negative** ●

How positive or negative an impression do you have of your country's tourists when they are in other countries? %

Country	Positive	Don't know	Negative
Great Britain	29	14	57
Norway	48	7	45
Germany	40	17	43
France	46	17	37
Italy	61	9	30
Australia	57	14	29
China	64	8	28
Saudi Arabia	61	11	27
USA	45	27	27
Kuwait	63	9	27
Egypt	67	10	23
Spain	66	11	22
Denmark	67	10	22
Vietnam	70	9	21
Sweden	58	20	21
Jordan	72	7	21
Singapore	72	10	18
Finland	71	13	17
Morocco	78	6	16
Malaysia	74	11	15
Indonesia	77	10	13
Thailand	77	11	12
UAE	82	6	12
Philippines	85	4	11
Oman	78	12	11
India	83	7	10

And how positive or negative an impression do you think the locals in other countries have of your countries tourists? %

Country	Positive	Don't know	Negative
Great Britain	23	16	61
Norway	30	16	54
Germany	36	17	47
France	42	11	47
Italy	45	11	44
Australia	35	24	42
China	55	10	35
Saudi Arabia	58	9	33
USA	53	14	32
Kuwait	56	14	30
Egypt	55	15	30
Spain	58	13	29
Denmark	54	18	28
Vietnam	61	14	25
Sweden	65	10	25
Jordan	60	17	23
Singapore	73	7	20
Finland	71	9	19
Morocco	64	18	18
Malaysia	75	7	18
Indonesia	71	12	17
Thailand	70	13	17
UAE	72	12	16
Philippines	75	10	15
Oman	83	4	13
India	72	16	12

Source: YouGov - 28 June - 21 August 2019

We are joined in this by the French (54% of whom think their own nation's holidaymakers are an irritant to the locals, compared to 30% who do not), Germans (47% versus 36%) and Norwegians (47% versus 42%).

Again, at the other end of the table, Filipinos are the most likely to think their tourists are greeted with a smile (83%).

Britons' belief that other countries take a dim view of our tourists is hardly unfounded. Asked to name up to three countries from which the worst tourists originate, almost half of Spanish people (46%) named Britain.

We also topped the list in Germany (39%) and also in our own country (23%). We in Britain are only marginally less likely to hold a negative view of American tourists (22%).

Also unpopular among Europeans are Russian tourists, particularly in Denmark, Sweden, Finland and Norway, where they top the list (at between 24% and 38% in each nation), as well as Germany where 36% of people named them among the world's worst tourists. Germans themselves were also frequently cited by other Europeans (including themselves) as being among the worst tourists, as were the Chinese.

Chinese tourists are even less popular in other parts of Asia (including China itself), being named as the worst tourists in Australia, Indonesia, Malaysia, the Philippines, Singapore, Thailand, and Vietnam. In fact an enormous 67% of Singaporeans included Chinese tourists in their list of the world's worst holidaymakers (they are also pretty unimpressed with Indian tourists, at 42%).

Asked where the best tourists come from, one nation stands out above all others: Japan. With Japanese football fans having made headlines around the world during the World Cup by helping to clean the stadiums after matches, the nation is consistently cited as being home to the most gladly received tourists the world over.

This is particularly the case in Finland, France, Germany, Indonesia, Malaysia, the Philippines, Singapore, and Thailand, all of whom placed Japanese tourists at the very top of their lists.

30 August 2019

From Barcelona to Malia: how Brits on holiday have made themselves unwelcome

The bad behaviour of British tourists abroad caused a surge in complaints to police in the Spanish city last year – but where else dreads their arrival?

By Homa Khaleeli

Is it something we said? If you are daydreaming about a summer holiday, you might get a less than warm welcome this year. This week, Barcelona became the latest tourist destination to hit back at British holidaymakers, blaming them for adding to a rise in complaints to police of almost a fifth last year, according to news reports.

Offences included drinking in the streets, all-night parties and getting naked in public – and totalled 113,707 between July and September. UK visitors avoiding countries targeted by terrorists created a tourist boom in Spain. But money can't buy you friends, it seems – with Brits regularly topping surveys of the nationality that locals least want to see propping up their bars. So where have we made ourselves unwelcome?

Spain

Aside from Barcelona, we are hardly more popular elsewhere in Spain – even the British hotspot of Majorca is cold-shouldering us. This summer, graffiti sprang up across the island's historic capital, Palma, reading 'Tourists go home' and 'Tourist, you are the terrorist'. The harsh words were said to be a response to the huge number of Brits now flooding the island. In 2014, things were even worse after the local mayor insisted he would take action when a teen was filmed performing an obscene act in public, sparking outrage. A year later, British police were sent to Magaluf and Ibiza to try to help local police with unruly tourists.

Greece

What's the problem with British tourists? The mayor of Malia was clear: 'They scream, they sing, they fall down, they take their clothes off, they cross-dress, they vomit,' he announced back in 2008. And, in case there was any question, he added: 'It is only the British people – not the Germans or the French.' By 2013, the situation was bad enough for the mayor to suggest creating an 'out-of-town' area for foreign holidaymakers, quickly dubbed a 'tourist ghetto'.

Latvia

The city of Riga is equally fed up with Brits behaving badly. Unsurprisingly, many in Latvia took exception at tourists urinating on the city's Freedom Monument, which honours soldiers killed while fighting for independence. 'If we also had other tourists, then British visitors who piss about all the time would not be as noticeable. Let's not be politically correct – unfortunately, this is their speciality,' the mayor said in 2009. One tourist information company said it had stopped dealing with British tourists altogether.

Malaysia

In 2015, a British tourist was accused of causing one of the country's deadliest earthquakes. A British woman – one of 10 tourists who stripped off on the top of Mount Kinabalu for a dare, to show they could withstand freezing conditions – was accused of angering the mountain, which is considered sacred by indigenous people. Four of the tourists were arrested for 'committing obscene acts in public', but later released with a fine after apologising.

The good news

According to the Foreign & Commonwealth Office's British Behaviour Abroad report, we are getting better. In the latest data, from 2014, there was a slight decrease in the numbers of British people arrested abroad in 2013/14. Most cases were handled in Spain (1,389), followed by the US (1,153) and the United Arab Emirates (261). Drug arrests had slightly increased from the year before (by 7%) but 'the number of cases remains low compared to recent years'.

17 January 2017

Overtourism: tackling the curse of too many tourists

By Emma Nolan

Continuously developing an understanding of the ECO issues most affecting our planet, the next step on our educational sustainability journey is to discuss one of the latest additions to the *Oxford Dictionary*.

Overtourism: *'the perceived overcrowding of an area from an excess of tourists, resulting in conflict with locals'*

Living in a world full of tourists who love to travel, explore and discover, did we ever stop to think about what impact our travels were having on the rest of the world?

What pushed tourism over the edge?

Alongside the rise of Instagram and its many image-based companions, the world of travel is now diluted with images of perfect beaches, picturesque trails and relaxing retreats not to be missed. In the tourist hotspots of Mallorca and Barcelona, they're even discussing the negative impact of the UNESCO's listing of World Heritage Sites. The argument is that although it works to preserve historic places, it destroys authenticity of communities and turns culture into theme park-style attractions.

Which areas are most affected?

One of the most famous places suffering from too many tourists is Venice. Blessed with just over 25 million visitors a year, the Venetian landscape is not only sinking underwater but its 60,000 strong local population is being washed away in a sea of boat tours and booze cruises.

Alongside Venice, an EU report last year stated that there were 105 worldwide destinations suffering from overtourism.

Symptoms of overtourism

One of the main concerns of overtourism is its alienation of local residents. This is due to rising rents, noise pollution and overcrowding on streets, in restaurants and in other local attractions. Alongside this there are also areas include that find their local shops to be displaced and heritage sites damaged due to an ever-increasing amount of footfall.

Once the initial symptoms set in, the tourist experience itself is degraded by crowds and longer queues. Then inevitably the problems seep down through to the overloading of local infrastructure including transportation of sewage, then onto the actual destruction or pollution of habitat such as in the Thai Islands where they continue to lose their coral reefs.

Residents setting limits

Recently graffiti messages surfaced in places such as Mallorca and Barcelona reading, 'One Flight Every Minute Is Not Sustainable' and 'Tourists Go Home, Refugees Welcome'.

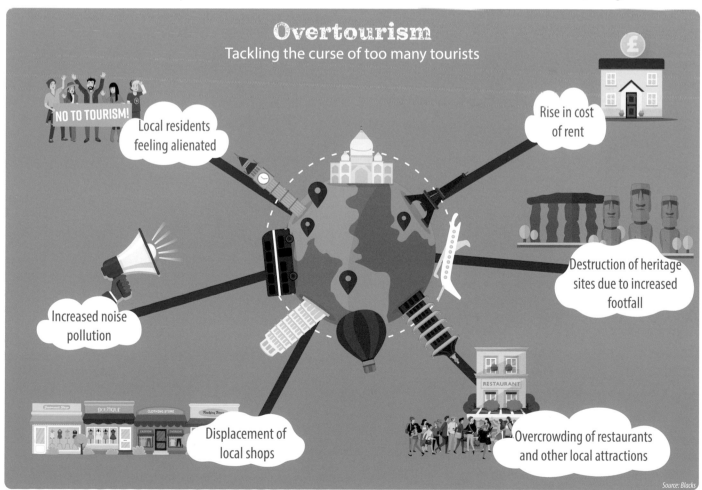

Overtourism
Tackling the curse of too many tourists

No to tourism!
Local residents feeling alienated
Rise in cost of rent
Increased noise pollution
Destruction of heritage sites due to increased footfall
Displacement of local shops
Overcrowding of restaurants and other local attractions

Source: Blacks

And, as tensions continue to grow, many nations want to take action.

Dubrovnik, Amsterdam and Santorini have all decided to limit the number of cruise ship passengers allowed to disembark each day. Alongside this, places such as Barcelona and Madrid are limiting lettings on Airbnb, whilst Venice plans to charge a day trippers fee of €2.50 in off-peak seasons and up to €10 during peak seasons.

Will this impact the tourism industry?

Tourism is actually one of the world's fastest growing industries and there looks to be no signs of slowing.

According to the World Travel & Tourism Council the industry accounts for 10% of the world's GDP.

However, Amsterdam and Paris now look to encourage tourism but have them holidaying in less-visited areas to drive interest away from busy cities and heritage sites.

As the industry struggles to cope it seems we must now not only consider the tourists but the locals too if we are to create a more sustainable tourism industry.

Overtourism: the problem with too much travel

By Caitlin Casey

In Paris, you'll find a mass of queues to go up and down the Eiffel Tower; in London, don't bother hitting up the London Eye unless you've booked; in New York, you'll be barging people out the way to make it to the middle of Times Square. It's no surprise that popular cities are a tourist's haven, but places like Phuket and Venice which were once remote and rural have now become packed with picture-taking and souvenir selling just as bad. So, what is this 'overtourism', and how detrimental has our travelling become?

You may have heard the word flung about in news articles and it had a steep increase of interest on Google towards the end of 2017; 'overtourism' refers to saturated areas of the world where the influx of tourist crowds has become so bad that they disturb the local community and environment.

Many cities throughout 2018 have had to address the overcrowding with some form of limitation to the area. Take the romantic getaway of Venice for example, where the mayor called for segregation between locals and tourists on a weekend in May this year by redirecting sightseers from the popular streets and certain areas only available to residents. But this isn't the first time Venice has had to make restrictions to tourists, when travellers were warned about 'sitting fines' in September 2017 of a fine up to 500 euros.

One of the problems with the industry is the exotic, luxurious ideal sold to travellers. Maya Bay in Thailand – which was once featured as a paradise destination in 2000 film *The Beach* – was reaching visitors of up to 5,000 a day back in June 2018 and saw a closure of four months to disperse the demand. Similarly, in the Philippines, the island of Boracay was reopened with strict limits on the tourism to regulate the excess population; restrictions were implemented such as no drinking and removal of casinos and beach vendors. Even all water sports were banned.

Not just the utopian paradise attractions are in danger of overtourism, the cultural and historical landmarks of cities bring in an excessive interest too. UNESCO World Heritage listings are often a child of overtourism because the historical connotations of the name automatically attract travellers – creating a catch 22 situation where environmental protection by UNESCO creates a consequential damage through human curiosity. Although managed and planned before being listed, there is a lack of funding and implementation to ensure that overtourism isn't a consequence of this title.

But can this problem be solved? If we filter tourism out to more remote places, surely this is just going to fill up the smaller, less-known adventures and make them just as full. Even if this overtourism averts travellers to far-flung escapes, many places which are unexplored can be dangerous. The city of Kyoto in Japan has been trying to ease off peak times from travellers who are putting themselves in danger with treacherous hikes and treks to get that perfect selfie.

There is one answer to this. Responsible tourism. A very simple answer to a big problem in the travel industry. To be able to responsibly travel is for us visitors to consider what the wider impacts are, and whether it can be made positive. Moving away from the typical landmarks and exploring cultures in different areas allows tourism to become more sustainable. With the uprise of 'ecotourism' and sustainable travel, it has become more accessible to travel without leaving a big mark.

So next time you're searching out the best hotspots on the next destination on your bucket list, crowded tourists and unsustainable impacts might not be so hot after all.

19 December 2018

Boom time for European tourism

A deep dive into the data behind the holiday business, with graphics and charts.

By Arnau Busquets Guàrdia

Tourism in Europe is booming – but not everyone is smiling in the sunshine.

Barcelona is trying to stop the construction of new hotels. The Louvre Museum in Paris had to close in May after staff went on strike over an 'unprecedented deterioration in visiting and working conditions' caused by ever-increasing crowds. Amsterdam launched the 'Enjoy and Respect' campaign and increased fines for drinking and urinating in public.

These three capitals were also among 10 European cities that this summer published a joint letter expressing concern about the 'explosive growth' of Airbnb and other holiday rental websites.

Worries about 'overtourism' are growing – but not many Europeans seem ready to forgo their summer holidays or weekend breaks, with EU residents now travelling more than ever. More than half of the bloc's citizens travel for pleasure every year.

Here's a visual deep dive into the data behind European tourism.

Taking off

After a drop caused by the economic crisis, the number of nights spent at tourist accommodation in the EU has increased steadily in recent years. It grew by 29.3% between 2009 and 2017

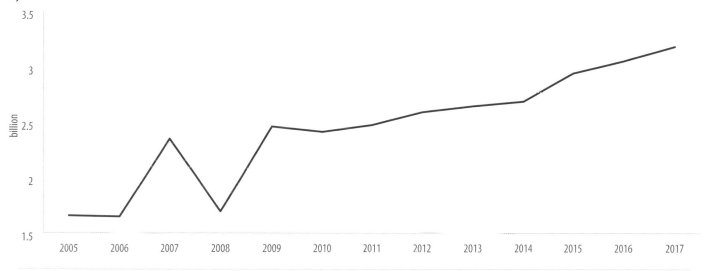

Some countries have seen a huge growth in tourism. Lithuania recorded four times more overnight stays in 2017 than in 2009. In the same period, Ireland has only seen a 2% growth. Increase in total nights stayed in tourist accommodation, including residents traveling within their home country, between 2009 and 2017:

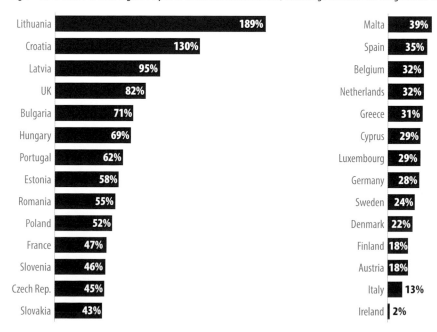

Lithuania 189%
Croatia 130%
Latvia 95%
UK 82%
Bulgaria 71%
Hungary 69%
Portugal 62%
Estonia 58%
Romania 55%
Poland 52%
France 47%
Slovenia 46%
Czech Rep. 45%
Slovakia 43%

Malta 39%
Spain 35%
Belgium 32%
Netherlands 32%
Greece 31%
Cyprus 29%
Luxembourg 29%
Germany 28%
Sweden 24%
Denmark 22%
Finland 18%
Austria 18%
Italy 13%
Ireland 2%

Hot spots

Spain is foreign tourists favourite EU destination. Nights spent by non-residents from all countries in 2017:

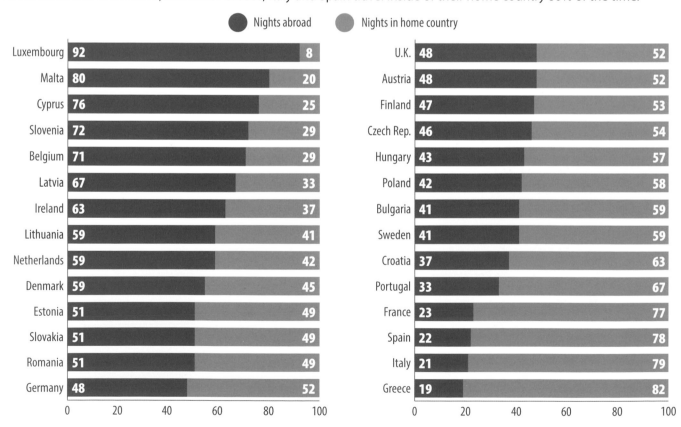

Spain	305,907,462
United Kingdom	279,453,070
Italy	210,658,786
France	133,499,991
Greece	89,284,390
Austria	86,044,321
Germany	83,111,219
Croatia	80,176,804
Portugal	48,884,842
Netherlands	44,169,040
Czech Rep.	26,257,013
Belgium	18,656,843
Bulgaria	17,105,567
Poland	16,705,215
Ireland	16,190,381
Cyprus	15,946,809
Hungary	14,941,781
Sweden	14,638,702
Denmark	11,914,787
Malta	9,184,161
Slovenia	8,478,019
Finland	6,742,834
Romania	5,267,970
Slovakia	5,316,945
Estonia	4,150,419
Latvia	305,907,462
Lithuania	3,431,233
Luxembourg	2,573,589

Top EU destinations for travellers from abroad

1 Canary Islands, ES: 93M
2 Adriatic Croatia, HR: 77M
3 Balearic Islands, ES: 64M
4 Catalonia, ES: 55M
5 Veneto, IT: 47M
6 Île de France, FR: 43M
7 Andalusia, ES: 38M
8 Tyrol, AT: 34M
9 West inner London, UK: 29M
10 East inner London, UK: 27M

Top EU destinations Including trips within own country

1 Canary Islands, ES: 104M
2 Catalonia, ES: 83M
3 Adriatic Croatia, HR: 82M
4 Île de France, FR: 80M
5 Balearic Islands, ES: 71M
6 Veneto, IT: 69M
7 Andalusia, ES: 69M
8 Provence-Alpes-C.Azur, FR: 52M
9 Valencia region, ES: 50M
10 Rhône-Alpes, FR: 49M

Far from home?

In terms of travel within the EU, Luxembourg's citizens spent nine out of 10 nights outside their home country in 2017. At the other end of the scale, citizens of Greece, Italy and Spain travel inside of their home country 80% of the time.

● Nights abroad   ● Nights in home country

Country	Nights abroad	Nights in home country
Luxembourg	92	8
Malta	80	20
Cyprus	76	25
Slovenia	72	29
Belgium	71	29
Latvia	67	33
Ireland	63	37
Lithuania	59	41
Netherlands	59	42
Denmark	59	45
Estonia	51	49
Slovakia	51	49
Romania	51	49
Germany	48	52
U.K.	48	52
Austria	48	52
Finland	47	53
Czech Rep.	46	54
Hungary	43	57
Poland	42	58
Bulgaria	41	59
Sweden	41	59
Croatia	37	63
Portugal	33	67
France	23	77
Spain	22	78
Italy	21	79
Greece	19	82

Source: Politico

Tourist takeover

How do tourist numbers compare with the number of residents in a country? In 2017, Malta and Croatia counted almost 20,000 overnight stays by foreign tourists for every 1,000 citizens living in the country.

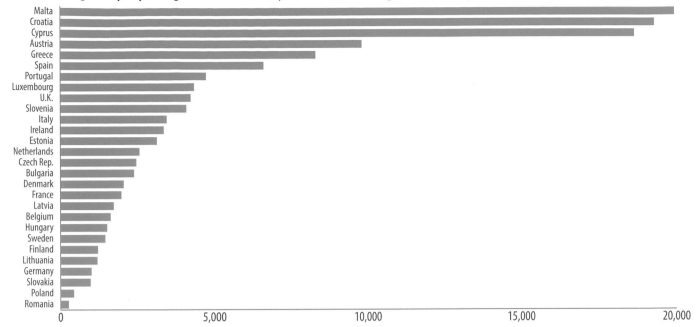

The bigger the country's population, the more tourists it hosts in tourist accomodations. But there are tourism overperformers (such as Spain, Malta and Croatia), and underperformers (such as Romania and Poland).

Hey, big spender

Not everyone in the EU travels as much. Nine in 10 Finnish citizens aged 15 or older participated in tourism for personal purposes in 2017.

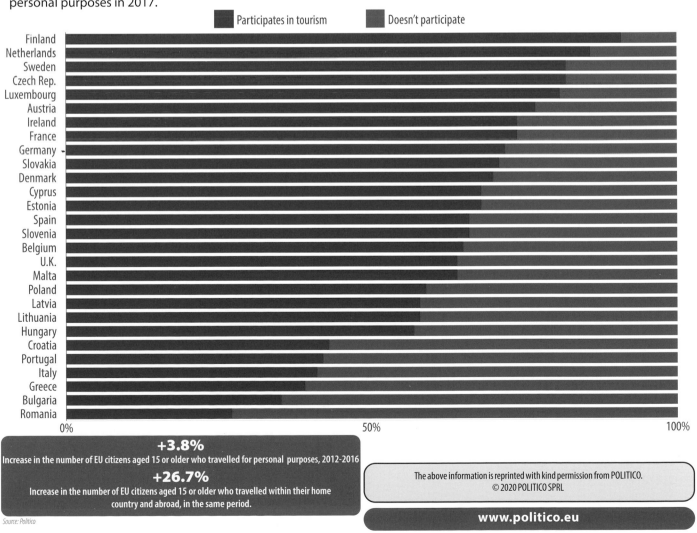

+3.8%
Increase in the number of EU citizens aged 15 or older who travelled for personal purposes, 2012-2016

+26.7%
Increase in the number of EU citizens aged 15 or older who travelled within their home country and abroad, in the same period.

Source: Politico

Why are we attracted to dark tourism?

By Samantha Wragg

Dark tourism isn't something new; however, it has only recently been given the official name after years of being a unique interest for certain travellers. Dark tourism is the act of travelling to a location that has an unusual or turbulent history and is a multi-million pound industry, with more and more travellers choosing to visit dark tourism locations every year.

Popularity of dark tourism

The growth in popularity has seen an increase in documentaries and various television shows around the topic of dark tourism, where hosts and presenters travel to some of the most popular locations and discover the troubled history for themselves. This has led to a further increase in travellers in these locations and sparked many a debate on whether dark tourism has a place in the world and why it's so popular.

Should dark tourism exist?

While some people may disagree, dark tourism absolutely has a place in the travel industry and does more good than it does harm. Not only does it bring these awful periods in history to light but only by providing the necessary education do we reduce the chances of disasters happening in the future and it is an important aspect of preserving and honouring the memories of those who needlessly suffered.

Of course, there are dark tourism sites that are run for negative reasons, usually just to earn a profit without care for the locals or those that lived through atrocities, but I've provided some suitable locations to inspire your next trip as a dark tourist.

London, United Kingdom

The capital of the UK and its most densely populated city, London is full of dark tales and mysterious history. Visit one of the many long-standing graveyards such as Highgate or Cross Bones, drop by the Tower of London where Guy Fawkes and Ann Boleyn lived their final days or learn something new on a historic walk around London's creepiest locations, where you can learn about the history of Jack the Ripper or chase the ghosts of London past.

Paris, France

Considered the country of love, France also hides some very dark secrets. In particular, the long-winding labyrinth of catacombs that reside below the city of Paris. Here, several million Parisians have been laid to rest, of which their bones can be seen lining the walls of the catacombs. Visits to the catacombs are expected to last an hour and tickets should be bought in advance as the location is one of the most popular in the world.

Amsterdam, Netherlands

Not only home to beautiful canals and what, at first glance, seems to be the whole world's supply of bicycles, the city of Amsterdam is also home to the Anne Frank House, another popular location with dark tourists from around the world. The Anne Frank House is where Anne Frank hid with her family from the Nazis during the Second World War and where she wrote her famous diary, the original of which is in the museum for visitors to see.

Pripyat, Ukraine

Ukraine is a beautiful country but is home to one of the world's most popular dark tourism sites – Chernobyl, the site of one of the world's worst nuclear accidents that took place in 1986. The nearest town of Pripyat remains a ghost town to this day and it's recorded that the area will remain unsafe for inhabitation for centuries to come. Visitors can take part in specially arranged tours across an area of 35km but must carry special devices that measure radiation in the air and prevent visitors wandering into potentially deadly radiation zones.

Travelling to a dark tourism site?

If you are planning on travelling to one of the above locations or planning a dark tourism journey of your own, make sure you behave appropriately. These locations, whilst they allow for photographs, are not somewhere you should be taking happy holiday snaps and you should be respectful of the history and those that lost their lives. As more tourists forget the rules and act inappropriately at these locations, we run the risk of losing these important historic destinations and preventing others from learning and helping to prevent disasters in the future.

5 September 2019

Why there's nothing wrong with being a tourist

By Cathy Adams

A few days ago, I read a worrying travel piece in the *Times of India* about North Sentinel – the remote Andaman island, flung off the eastern coast of India, inhabited by tribes entirely untouched by the modern world. You might remember the story of missionary John Allen Chau, who travelled to the protected island last year to spread Christianity, only to be killed by tribes people.

Suffice to say it's not anywhere that should be on anyone's bucket list, whatever kind of traveller they are.

'If you're an adventurous soul and want to explore the unknown, a visit to North Sentinel Island can be an option,' the (now edited) piece trilled. 'You can become the next Columbus and let the world know about your adventurous travel. Or, just get hunted by spears!'

How have we got to this point? Where the only travel experiences worth writing about involve (probable) death?

I've got one answer: disdain for the bread-and-butter tourist.

There's an advert on the London Underground at the moment, advertising the Royal Museums Greenwich. One poster image shows a girl jumping high above the meridian line with the tagline: 'Don't be a tourist. Be an explorer.' As if stomping up the hill to the Royal Observatory in Greenwich Park was on the same level as Edmund Hillary and Tenzing Norgay scaling Everest (I mean, it is rather a big hill). The Greenwich museum even advertises itself as 'a top 10 visitor attraction in London' – but for some reason sniffs at the idea that it might welcome a tourist or two.

I posted a picture of the advert on Twitter last week, asking if the word 'tourist' had become a dirty word. Most of the responses were full of contempt for this type of snobbery and resignation for this new breed of 'explorer'.

The stereotype of the tourist, especially in Britain's case – hewn on the beaches of southern Spain and Greece, blown into popular culture two decades ago when commercial flights became cheap enough for everyone to travel – has become a mucky one. It assumes you want to spend your holiday blithely taking photos and marching through museum gift shops without really, howl, 'getting under the skin of a place'. And you'll probably be wearing socks and sandals and drinking a happy-hour cocktail.

Tourism hasn't been helped by being constantly prefixed by 'over': a modern phenomenon which has blighted cities and regions around the world including Barcelona, Amsterdam, Kyoto and Venice.

But it's left this weird legacy that suggests if you want to travel, you should consistently seek the under-the-radar, the quirky, the unnoticed things. It means you need to somehow blend in with the locals and pretend to not be an outsider. Which is wild, because we're all outsiders when it comes to it, aren't we? It's cultural snobbery to suggest that the 4.4 billion people who boarded planes in 2018 were 'discoverers' rather than, I don't know, sitting on the beach reading a book.

We've written before about the joy of being an outsider in a city. Why the idea of 'living like a local' is a total fantasy. 'There's a reason why walking the remnants of the Berlin Wall, or tours of the Roman Forum, or ogling the Sagrada Familia are popular,' writes David Whitley. 'They're amazing, well worth travelling to and not available anywhere else. If you're going somewhere for a weekend, it's entirely sane and logical to concentrate on things that are genuinely unique to that place.'

Being a tourist also means ditching the identikit Brooklyn-esque restaurants with bare-brick walls and Edison lamps. Relief!

Often, the mass experiences that are sneeringly dubbed 'touristy' are popular because... they're good. Climbing the Sydney Harbour Bridge (expensive but worth it) was an epic experience. Bobbing across Hong Kong's Victoria Harbour for about 20 pence on the Star Ferry, watching the neon skyscrapers light up the clouds, is top on TripAdvisor for a reason. There are few places you can learn as much about European art as in the Louvre (yes, I know the queues are ridiculous and the *Mona Lisa* is much smaller than you'd think).

As Mark Jones writes today in *The Independent,* some of the world's most special travel experiences are those that are shared by millions of others: the Valley of the Kings, Paris' Latin Quarter, Uluru at sunset.

Of course, there are ways to be a tourist and to travel responsibly with good grace. Think twice about going on a cruise ship to Venice. If you want to visit Amsterdam, why not stay in nearby Rotterdam for a third of the price and take the (20-minute) train instead? And Osaka has a much better vibe than crammed Kyoto, let's be honest.

Plus, being a tourist allows you to plough money into the places that really need it. Tourism contributed $8.8 trillion to the world economy in 2018, with 319 million people employed in the industry according to figures from the World Travel & Tourism Council. That's almost one in 15 people worldwide. Are you still ashamed of being a tourist?

Let's indulge in being tourists, in the joy of the shared experience, the eye of the outsider. My next trip is to Greece, where I plan to visit the Acropolis and spend all day at a beach club in Mykonos. And there's absolutely nothing wrong with that.

29 August 2019

1% of English residents take one-fifth of overseas flights, survey shows

FoI request to DfT reveals 10% most frequent flyers took more than half of flights abroad in 2018.

By Niko Kommenda

Just 1% of English residents are responsible for nearly a fifth of all flights abroad, according to previously unpublished statistics.

The figures, published in a Department for Transport survey, also reveal that the 10% most frequent flyers in England took more than half of all international flights in 2018. However, 48% of the population did not take a single flight abroad in the last year.

The new findings bolster calls for a frequent flyer levy, a proposal under which each citizen would be allowed one tax-free flight per year but would pay progressively higher taxes on each additional flight taken.

The revelations follow a new report from the Committee on Climate Change (CCC), the government's official adviser, which urged ministers to put tougher regulations on the international aviation and shipping sectors to keep the economy on track for net-zero carbon emissions by 2050.

Environmental activists said the new figures showed the UK could cut air traffic and emissions without affecting ordinary holidaymakers.

'There is this narrative that tackling the climate change problem from aviation means stopping people from taking holidays or seeing their families – and actually, when you look at this data that is wrong,' said Leo Murray, director of innovation at 10:10 Climate Action.

'What we need to do is target a minority of problem flyers and stop them from taking so many flights,' he added.

The findings are based on responses from more than 15,000 English residents who participated in the 2018 National Transport Survey and were revealed to *The Guardian* following a Freedom of Information request.

The aviation sector accounted for about 7% of the UK's total greenhouse gas emissions in 2017. It is projected to be the single biggest source of emissions in the UK by 2050 due to the steadily increasing demand for flights.

John Sauven, executive director of Greenpeace UK, also endorsed the idea of a frequent flyer levy. 'It makes it easier for families to fly once a year, but the escalating tax on further flights means that the people responsible for most of the problem are the ones who end up paying most of the tax – or, ideally, flying a lot less,' he said.

In England last year 1% of people took nearly one-fifth of all flights abroad

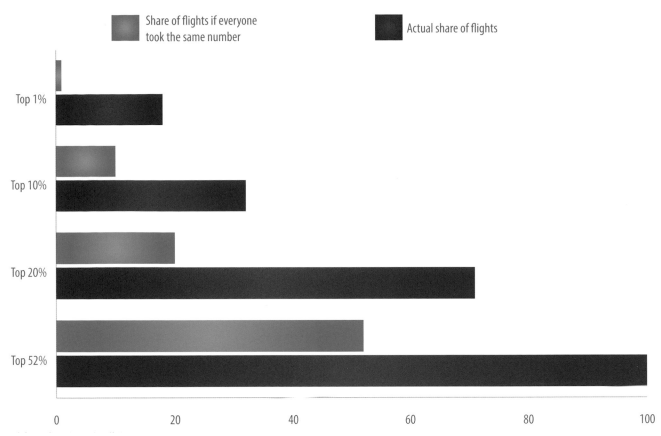

Share of flights if everyone took the same number

Actual share of flights

Siân Berry, co-leader of the Green party, said the new data showed the UK could cut its air traffic without hitting those who can least afford it. 'It's about people who fly again and again and again.'

'A progressive tax on the most frequent flyers is a fair policy that most people would come behind if the government put it forward,' she added.

Tuesday's CCC report suggested a number of policy options to curb demand for flights, including a frequent flyer levy, and said technological improvements alone could not be the solution to the growing emissions problem. There is currently no country in which travellers pay an escalating levy on each flight they take in a year.

'In the absence of a true zero-carbon plane, demand cannot continue to grow unfettered over the long-term,' it stated.

Emissions from international aviation are not currently included in national carbon budgets such as the UK's but instead managed by a dedicated UN agency – the International Civil Aviation Organization (ICAO). However, some have said the body is too secretive and close to industry to take on the major polluters.

The CCC said international air travel should be included in the UK's climate strategy like any other business sector.

'Not having [international aviation] in the target is a barrier to putting in place good policies to get us on the trajectory

to be net-zero overall,' said Chris Stark, the CCC's chief executive.

He argued that the UK should take a leading role in cutting emissions from the sector, rather than wait for more comprehensive international agreements to be struck.

'There should be no barrier to bringing aviation emissions into the carbon budgets and then putting in place a set of policies that at some stage in the future will be compatible with those international agreements,' Stark said.

A DfT spokesperson said: 'Tackling climate change is one of the most urgent and pressing challenges that we face. Which is why this government has set a bold 2050 net zero target for the UK and a greener aviation industry will play a key role in that.

'The government is funding the future of flight and have announced £5 million in funding for new technologies like electric and autonomous aircraft to help us tackle climate change. We are working with our partners to ensure the government takes a leading role in reducing greenhouse gas emissions in the aviation sector.'

25 September 2019

Two-thirds of people support limiting air travel to tackle climate change

Addressing climate change requires a 'high' or 'extremely high' level of urgency, say more than three in five people.

Two-thirds of people also support limiting air travel in order to address climate change, whilst just over half are in support of reducing the amount of meat in our diets.

This is according to results from a YouGov poll commissioned by a brand new UK research centre set up to examine the social and behavioural changes needed for a low-carbon and sustainable society.

Led by scientists from Cardiff University, the Centre for Climate Change and Social Transformations (CAST) will explore ways in which people can act directly to reduce their own carbon emissions, as well as influence other people, organisational decisions, and policies.

The centre has also been praised by climate activist Greta Thunberg who, in a special recorded message, described CAST as 'extremely important and essential' to helping achieve the drastic changes in our lifestyles to combat the climate crisis.

The £5 million ESRC-funded centre is a collaboration between Cardiff, Manchester, York and East Anglia Universities, as well as the charity Climate Outreach.

Launching today at a special event held at Cardiff University, the Centre aims to become a global hub for understanding the profound changes required to address climate change, with a focus on four areas: food and diet; transport and mobility; consumption of goods; and heating and cooling.

To coincide with the launch, new findings have been released from research carried out in August 2019 assessing the public perceptions of climate change in the UK.

A total of 2,018 people were surveyed, which revealed that the urgency of climate change was recognised by the majority of respondents.

- More than three out of five people (62%) said that addressing climate change requires a 'high' or 'extremely high' level of urgency.

- A majority (61%) supported the UK Parliament's declaration of a 'climate emergency', with only 11% opposing this.

- Two-thirds of people (67%) felt that we should limit air travel in order to address climate change, whereas only 22% felt we do not need to do so.

- Just over half of the respondents (53%) were of the view that we should reduce the amount of meat in our diets to address climate change, whereas 37% felt we do not need to do so.

Professor Lorraine Whitmarsh, Director of the Centre for Climate Change and Social Transformations said: 'We are very excited to be launching CAST. The Centre will aim to put people at the heart of the transformations required to address climate change, and seek to find ways in which we can live better as well as in low-carbon and sustainable ways.

'Cardiff University, together with our partners in Manchester, East Anglia, and York Universities, and charity Climate Outreach, will be working with a range of private-, public- and third-sector partners to understand how to transform lifestyles, organisations and social structures in order to achieve a low-carbon future.

'Our new survey findings make clear that most people feel climate change is an urgent issue, and are willing to make significant changes to their own lifestyles to help tackle it. Changing travel and food habits are amongst the most impactful thing individuals can do to reduce their carbon footprint – it's very encouraging that there's support amongst the public for making these changes.'

Professor Jennifer Rubin, executive chair of the Economic and Social Research Council, said: 'This is a really important Centre to be funding because of its strong focus on developing and testing effective approaches to communicating climate change and its effects. Despite the urgent need to tackle climate change, researchers know that people rarely talk about it on a day-to-day basis – this means opportunities for meaningful dialogue and practical responses relevant to people's everyday lives are missed.'

At the Centre's launch, speakers from Cardiff University, the Economic and Social Research Council, and National Assembly for Wales shared their views on how people can live differently in ways that meet the urgent need for rapid and far-reaching emission reductions.

18 September 2019

Global tourism leaves a giant carbon footprint

By Daniel T. Cross

We all love to travel. Many of us do at any rate. We love to explore, discover new places, make new friends and get acquainted with cultures different from our own. It's all harmless fun, after all.

Or is it?

No, it's not, according to an international team of researchers. The carbon footprint of global tourism is way larger than previously assumed, they say. The researchers conducted a global survey of 160 countries between 2009 and 2013 in order to calculate the amount of CO2 emissions produced by the tourism industry worldwide.

In so doing, they scanned more than a billion supply chains with the aim of tracking the goods and services tourists bought. What they found was that the tourism industry's carbon footprint around the planet grew by 15% from 3.9 to 4.5 gigatons of equivalent carbon dioxide. That is four times more than previously thought and accounted for about 8% of global greenhouse gas emissions in the surveyed period.

'Transport, shopping and food are significant contributors,' they explain, writing in the journal *Nature Climate Change*. 'The majority of this footprint is exerted by and in high-income countries. The rapid increase in tourism demand is effectively outstripping the decarbonisation of tourism-related technology.'

And it's going to get worse. Tourism is a trillion-dollar industry that is expected to grow by 4% each year, faster than international trade. The growth is largely a result of increasing wealth creation in countries like China where more and more people can now travel for leisure.

The researchers project that 'due to its high carbon intensity and continuing growth, tourism will constitute a growing part of the world's greenhouse gas emissions'. They estimate that global tourism will increase carbon emissions to about 6.5Gt by 2025. Currently, the United States produces most of the tourism-related emissions, followed by China, Germany and India.

On a per-capita basis, however, it's small island nations popular with tourists that have the largest carbon footprints, the researchers explain. '[The] Maldives tops the list – 95% of the island's tourism-related emissions come from international visitors,' they write. 'Tourists are responsible for 30–80% of the national emissions of island economies.'

A solution for reducing the industry's massive carbon footprint lies in responsible tourism. 'Ultimately real change will come from implementing regulations and incentives together to encourage low-carbon operations,' the researchers argue.

'At a personal level, though, it's worth looking at the carbon-cost of your flights, choosing to offset your emissions where possible and supporting tourism companies that aim to operate sustainably,' they add.

10 September 2019

The impacts of 'eco-tourism'

Everyone needs a good vacation. Eco-friendly travel can affect not only how to travel but also where on the planet people travel.

By Emily Folk

The eco-tourism movement has continued to impact where people choose to spend their vacations.

Eco-tourism serves to promote increased environmental awareness, sustainable communities, cultural experiences and environmental preservation and conservation.

Yet the inherent nature of tourism demands that there be developments, which haven't always benefited the environment. Nevertheless, for those planning a sustainable vacation, it's important to keep eco-tourist considerations in mind.

Eco-tourism benefits

With eco-tourism comes curiosity – about both environment and experience. Instead of going to popular tourist destinations like China, Italy, Spain and Germany, vacationers are expanding their searches and destinations.

More destinations mean more opportunities for employment within indigenous populations of lower-income communities and countries. Locals act as guides, experts, demonstrators, merchants and hosts to visiting tourists. Increased traffic means more money funnelling directly back into the community along with a higher standard of living.

Community outreach and tourism allow people from all over the world to come into an impoverished community and restore it by providing services and patronage. In one instance, a vacation could mean volunteering, building or serving in an impoverished community. Another impact would come from immersive experiences in the lives of indigenous peoples that sustain their culture and environment.

Eco-tourism also provides cultural literacy. By incorporating local cultural lodging, food, history and activities, communities can improve their welfare as well as educate a wider population.

Plus, taking some press away from the typical tourist destinations means that some pressure is taken off the surrounding environment and ecosystems. The money that results and is saved from releasing the environmental pressures is put back into conservation and preservation efforts.

Negative developments

With increased tourism comes increased pressure to develop areas and make them more inclusive and resort-like. Building more accommodation, businesses and amenities within these communities and destinations damages and destroys habitats. By damaging the local environment, you increase the pressure on native species.

Increased competition for resources between invading tourist activity and indigenous populations – both locals and

wildlife – means wildlife and certain ways of life disappear. In their place, these cultures and environments take on the same features and characteristics of previous popular sites.

Indigenous cultures are distorted to consumer culture to keep tourists coming, which leads to the exploitation of resources and wildlife that's currently destroying destinations like the Bahamas and the Philippines.

Not all eco-tourist destinations are what they appear to be. Some eco-tourists book vacations thinking they're going to have an authentic, sustainable experience when that's not the case.

Even cycling and hiking close to home can have devastating effects on the environment and wildlife. While vacation should be an enjoyable and memorable experience, the environment is not to be exploited for a stellar photo album.

Thankfully, instances of irresponsible excursions such as reckless mountain biking and enclosing wildlife for display and hunting have diminished.

Vacation impact

Eco-tourism calls on vacationers to redefine what it means to take a vacation – not only where you go and how you get there, but also what you do while you're there.

This strategy affects how people choose where to stay. With home-sharing sites like Airbnb growing more popular with five million listings worldwide, many people are opting for a more cost-effective, authentic experience for their vacations. (Airbnb has itself been criticised because of its impact on local communities and economies.)

There's also been an increase in the demand for energy-efficient hotels and resorts that benefit the local cultures as well as the environment. Food is something that everyone should consider as well. Trying the local dishes and delicacies is part of every vacation, and you're supporting the local farmers when you buy from local vendors.

With immersion in the homes and lifestyles of the cultures surrounding you, you can grow to appreciate them and the environment more. It also makes you more curious about what else is out there. With local guides, you'll realise how many activities are available that wouldn't be found in a resort.

Eco-tourism is often close to home too. A study of 160 countries found that tourism accounts for eight percent of the world's carbon emissions and is increasing each year. If you're worried about the effects of your travelling, consider a low-carbon vacation, which means foregoing the standard airfare travel and road trip in favour of one closer to your own backyard. Instead of staying at a hotel, it can mean camping, climbing, hiking, backpacking or biking.

Eco-destinations

If you already know what you're looking for, go somewhere that's likely to give you the right experience. Here are some common goals for travelling as well as corresponding destinations:

- ◆ **For the community and culture:** Cambodia, India, Kenya and Ethiopia

- ◆ **For the conservationist efforts:** South Africa, Belize, Malawi and Thailand

- ◆ **For the outdoors:** Peru, Argentina and the United States

- ◆ **For the history:** Japan, Jordan, Ethiopia and Vietnam

- ◆ **For the wildlife:** Finland, Canada, the Azores, India, Borneo and Uganda

Eco-tourism tips

For the best experience with eco-tourism, consider the following tips:

- ◆ **Do your research:** When it comes to taking a sustainable vacation, make sure all the details are spelled out. Do some research into the company you're staying with, the excursions you'd like to go on and the places you're visiting.

- ◆ **Avoid taking more than you need:** Whether you're going abroad or just camping on a local mountain, a light suitcase or backpack will complement a high sense of adventure. When you're packing for a hike or a flight, remember to keep it quick, easy and light, including the clothes you wear, the tools you use and the food you eat.

- ◆ **Always keep the environment in mind:** As long as you're keeping the health of the environment in mind when you plan your vacation, you'll be doing your part as a responsible traveller.

Eco-tourism has had an impact on the way people think about leisure and how they feel about vacation. Fun doesn't have to be sacrificed for sustainability and a greener planet. In fact, these lifestyles open up more opportunities to see the world and make every vacation an adventure.

18 January 2019

What are the negative effects of tourism on the environment?

Unsustainable tourism can have significant negative effects on the environment of a region.

Tourism is usually regarded as a boon to a region's economy. Tourism brings prosperity to the region and provides employment to the locals of the region. However, when tourism becomes unsustainable in nature, it can have disastrous consequences on the environment. When the tourist industry active in the region crosses the legal and ethical barriers to earn more profit, it can lead to massive degradation of the environment in the area. Local human population, flora and fauna, suffer greatly due to such irresponsible and unsustainable tourism. Some of the ways in which tourism adversely impacts the environment have been mentioned below:

Tourism and pollution

Transport of tourists results in air pollution

The movement of tourists from their home to the tourist destination involves transport via road, rail, or air, or a combination of these modes of transport. When a large number of tourists are involved, it invariably leads to a greater use of the transportation system. We all are aware of the fact that emissions from automobiles and airplanes are one of the biggest causes of air pollution. When a large number tourists use these modes of transport to reach a particular attraction, it pollutes the air both locally and globally. Due to the rapid growth in international tourism, tourists now account for nearly 60% of air travel. In many places, buses or other vehicles leave their motors running to ensure that tourists return to comfortable air-conditioned vehicles. Such practices further pollute the air.

Tourism leads to noise pollution

Tourist destinations are often subject to significant noise pollution. Tourist vehicles entering and leaving natural areas create a lot of noise. Such noise is the source of distress for wildlife. Loud music played by tourists in forested areas also disturb the animals living in the area. Often, noise generated by tourist activities for long-term alters the natural activity patterns of animals.

Littering of tourist spots by irresponsible tourists

Irresponsible tourists often litter the tourist spots visited by them. Waste disposal is a great problem in the natural environment. According to estimates, cruise ships in the Caribbean produce over 70,000 tons of waste annually. If waste is disposed of irresponsibly in the sea, it can lead to the death of marine animals. Even Mount Everest is not free of human-generated waste. Trekkers leave behind their oxygen cylinders, garbage, and camping equipment on the mountains and hills. Some trails in the Himalayas and the Andes have been nicknamed the 'Toilet paper trail' or the 'Coca-Cola trail', referring to the garbage left behind on such trails.

Sewage generated at tourist spots contaminate the natural environment

Rampant construction of tourist facilities like hotels, cafes, restaurants, etc., in an area without proper arrangement for safe disposal of sewage, can lead to disastrous consequences. Wastewater carrying sewage from such areas often pollutes nearby water bodies. It can lead to the eutrophication of water bodies and the loss of the balance in aquatic ecosystems. Pollution of water bodies with sewage can also lead to health issues and even epidemics that can ultimately wipe out large populations of aquatic flora and fauna and also impact human health adversely.

Tourism can spoil the aesthetics of the environment

Tourist facilities built to earn a profit without any concern about integrating the design with the natural features of the place can lead to aesthetic pollution. Large resorts of disparate designs can dominate the landscape and spoil the natural beauty of a place.

Tourism and natural resources

When tourism is encouraged in an area with inadequate resources, it will have a negative impact on the ecosystem of the area. In such areas, the local flora and fauna might be deprived of the resources needed to sustain their lives. For example, large volumes of water are consumed to cater to the needs of the tourists, run hotels, swimming pools, maintain golf courses, etc. This can degrade the quality of water and decrease the volume of water that is available for the local population, plants, and animals. It is not only the water resources that are depleted. Unsustainable practices by the tourist industry can also put pressure on other resources like food, energy, etc.

Tourism and physical degradation of the ecosystem

Every ecosystem works on a delicate natural balance. Every species in the ecosystem has a specific role to play in the system. However, tourism often disturbs this delicate balance and creates a great disaster in the ecosystem. When the tourist industry active in an area is completely profit-minded, it pays little heed to the needs of nature. For example, often hotels and resorts are built illegally very close to the beach or inside the core areas of forests. Large patches of natural vegetation need to be cleared to allow space for the sprawling resorts or hotels. As old tourist spots get degraded due to overuse by tourists, newer 'upcoming' destinations with fewer crowds become the next favourite of tourists and the tourism industry. The same situation is repeated once more. Unsustainable practices by the tourism industry can thus lead to deforestation, sand erosion, loss of species, changes in sea currents and coastlines, destruction of habitats, etc. Even activities like nature walks can be harmful to the environment if tourists trample on the local vegetation during their walk. Such trampling can lead to reduced plant vigour, breakage of stems, reduced regeneration, etc. Tourists breaking off corals during snorkelling or scuba diving activities can also contribute to ecosystem degradation. Commercial harvesting of corals for sale to tourists also causes harm to coral reefs. Even the anchorage of cruise ships to coral reefs can degrade large sections of the reef.

11 October 2018

Tourists cause 40% spike in plastic entering Mediterranean Sea each summer, report finds

'When we come home with our happy memories, we're leaving behind a toxic legacy of plastic waste.'

By Josh Gabbatiss

Every summer the holidaymakers hitting the beaches of the Mediterranean bring with them a massive wave of marine litter.

A new report released by WWF has revealed tourists cause a 40 per cent surge in waste entering the Mediterranean Sea, 95 per cent of which is plastic.

Among the worst offenders for plastic pollution were Turkey, Spain, Italy, Egypt and France – countries more than 34 million British people are set to visit this year.

The plastic waste is threatening the region's wildlife, with reports of whales dying after consuming plastic bags and tuna found with stomachs full of cellophane.

Though the Mediterranean has received less attention than the infamous 'garbage patches' that form in major oceans, it has been described by scientists as one of the regions most threatened by marine litter.

'Levels of microplastics found in the Mediterranean were nearly four times higher than found in the North Pacific "plastic island",' Lyndsey Dodds, head of marine policy at WWF, told *The Independent*.

While the Mediterranean holds only 1% of the world's water, it contains 7% of all of the world's microplastic waste.

'Many factors make this the case,' explained Dr David Barnes of the British Antarctic Survey, whose research contributed to the WWF report.

'The Mediterranean is a region of high multiple anthropogenic stresses so plastic interacts and compounds these to make life there especially vulnerable.'

Besides being fed by densely populated and highly industrialised waterways, the Mediterranean acts as a trap for plastics from further afield.

Plastics accumulate in the semi-enclosed sea in huge quantities, where they break down into smaller and smaller fragments over long periods of time.

'Increasingly, degradation and sinking of plastics mean that what was once a sea surface and beach strand issue has become much bigger and less visible by accumulating on the seabed, into more remote locations and into the foodweb,' Dr Barnes told *The Independent*.

WWF's tips for avoiding plastic waste on holiday

When shopping for souvenirs use a bag for life

Think twice about buying that inflatable pool toy

Bring your own water bottle

Enjoy a plastic-free drink without straws or stirrers

Check out the local recycling when renting a property

Microplastics – tiny fragments that can come from cosmetics, clothing or the degradation of larger plastics – have become a ubiquitous menace, with samples of sea ice from both poles revealing traces of them.

'I think it's fair to say that the more we look for microplastics the more we find them – and see this is a problem everywhere,' said Ms Dodds.

Though scientists are not clear about the impact of microplastics, there is concern that they will accumulate in the food chain and result in health issues for animals and potentially humans.

This appears to be playing out in the fin whales of the Pelagos Sanctuary in the northwestern Mediterranean.

The tissue of these giant mammals has levels of phthalates – potentially harmful chemicals that result from the breakdown of plastics – that are five times higher than whales sampled from less contaminated regions.

Besides the 130,000 tons of microplastics thought to end up in the sea from Europe every year, the report – released to mark World Oceans Day – found that the region dumps as much as 500,000 tons of larger plastics.

This volume, which is the equivalent of 66,000 full rubbish trucks, poses a major threat to marine creatures, which can become entangled in plastic debris or consume it after mistaking it for food.

According to the report, Europe has become one of the largest plastic producers in the world – second only to China.

'The Mediterranean is a beautiful holiday destination enjoyed by millions of British people each summer but when we come home with our happy memories, we're leaving behind a toxic legacy of plastic waste,' said Tanya Steele, chief executive at WWF.

'The birds, fish, and turtles of the Mediterranean are choking on plastic, but our report also shows plastic is ending up in the fish and seafood we eat on holiday.

'That's why we're asking people to think about how they can cut down on the amount of single-use plastic they use and throw away on holiday.'

Besides asking individuals to be mindful of their plastic consumption on holiday, the environmental organisation is urging Mediterranean governments to take immediate action on plastics.

'Each of the countries need to bring in their own targets to try and achieve 100 percent of waste being recycled or reusable by 2030 under the EU targets – and also to consider bans on particular items,' said Ms Dodds.

'In the UK specifically we are asking for a ban on particular items where alternatives are readily available – things like straws, stirrers, cutlery, as well as taxes on a range of other products.'

However, the Mediterranean is more than just Europe, and Dr Barnes noted that poverty and governance issues mean many of the region's bordering countries may not consider the issue of plastic pollution to be significant.

WWF has also emphasised the importance of greater responsibility falling on producers and retailers, so they are obliged to oversee the full life cycle of all their plastics.

7 June 2018

Tourism is damaging the ocean. Here's what we can do to protect it

By Jemi Laclé, Project Manager, Data and Analytics, Energy and Extractives Global Practice, World Bank Group, Aleksandra Dragozet, Founder & CEO, Sea Going Green & Melissa Novotny, Business and Partnership Development Manager, Sea Going Green

What does the big blue mean to you? Is it a holiday destination, a source of income, as for the 60 million people working in the marine fishing industry, a vital protein source of 151 million tonnes for human consumption, or a home to millions of species? The ocean has a different meaning for everyone, but for all of us, it is a source of life.

Vitamin sea

It is often forgotten that two-thirds of the Earth's surface is covered by water. The ocean is big, resilient and heals the soul, but what happens when it is facing a crisis and cannot revitalise its own wounds? Scientists are predicting that 90% of the world's coral reefs will die by 2050 and that the ocean's biodiversity is degrading at an alarming pace, due to human activities.

With a growing global middle class and increasing ease of travel, people have achieved greater mobility in recent years. According to United Nations World Tourism Organization, the number of international tourist trips worldwide reached 1.3 billion in 2017, and is predicted to reach 1.8 billion by 2030.

The World Travel Tourism Council forecasts that the future of travel and tourism will support 400 million jobs and contribute to 25% of global net job creation globally. The infrastructure required to sustain this growth in economic activity has increased pressure on natural resources, biodiversity, as well as on local communities.

Tourism can cause harm, but it can also stimulate sustainable development. When properly planned and managed, sustainable tourism can contribute to improved livelihoods, inclusion, cultural heritage and natural resource protection, and promote international understanding.

Here are three examples of how tourism is harming our oceans, and the efforts to mitigate that harm:

1. The cost of tourism

Various tourist hotspots struggle to manage the ever-expanding influx of travellers. Urban dwellers in cities like Amsterdam, Venice and Barcelona are raising their concerns and anti-tourist sentiment is growing. Tourism-driven gentrification can put pressure on the wellbeing and livelihood of the local community, pushing up real estate prices, making the destination overcrowded, and enhancing shore erosion by tourist activities in coastal areas.

In 2017, Palau and New Zealand started a bold campaign requesting visitors to be environmental agents by signing an eco-pledge when visiting their countries. This small step

Quick reef facts

Value of coral reefs per year (USD)

$35,473,669,000

Total visitation value

68,563,704

Highest value reefs (top 10%) generate

>$908,000 per km² per year

249,243 km² Total reef area

73,532 km² (29%) Reefs used for tourism

Source: Mapping Ocean Ecosystem Services, 2018

On reef tourism (diving, snorkelling, glass-bottom boats): $19,374,449,000 — 54%

Adjacent reef tourism (beaches, calm seas, views, seafood): $16,099,220,000 — 45%

Millions, US Dollars

is crucial to shift visitors' behaviour towards respecting the culture, protecting the country's natural and living resources, and preserving the country for future generations.

Awareness of sustainability is more important than ever, as user-generated content and peer-to-peer digital platforms like Instagram, Facebook, Airbnb and TripAdvisor are becoming key influencers of the experience economy, tourism trends, and the attitudes of globetrotters.

2. Toxic sunscreen in our seas

As the number of beachgoers has been growing, so has the use of sun protection products. Many people are unaware but 14,000 tonnes of toxic sunscreen make their way to the underwater world each year. In fact, as many as 82,000 kinds of chemicals from personal care products end up in the oceans. The use of chemical sunscreen, water pollution, coral diseases, rising sea temperatures and ocean acidification, lead to deformations in juvenile corals, bleaching of reefs and prevent corals from growing, reproducing and surviving.

In 2018, Hawaii, Mexico and Aruba announced a ban on non-biodegradable sunscreen lotions. Seychelles took a step further and committed to a blue bond to support the financing of ocean and marine-based projects for positive economic, environmental and climate benefits. It is key to have a holistic and innovative approach to the blue economy as the industry is expected to grow at twice the rate of the mainstream economy by 2030.

3. Circular tides

Global awareness of the footprint of (micro)plastic from tourism gained momentum in 2018. Researchers estimate that an additional eight million metric tonnes of plastic ends up in the ocean every year. About 40% of all plastic is in single-use packaging, as tourists litter beaches with straws, coffee cups, water bottles and cigarette butts.

In October 2018, Thailand announced the closing of Maya Beach indefinitely to clean up the unstoppable amount of plastic and drainage that tarnished its coastline. The threat to our oceans requires cross-country and regional collaboration, but most importantly multi-stakeholder global engagements.

Strategic partnerships empowering the public and private sector to reduce plastic waste, develop a circular economy and build sustainable and more resilient communities are critical. The alliance between the world's largest packaging producers, like the New Plastics Economy Global Commitment are key to forging innovative collective action, and solutions to reducing pollution to save our oceans.

There are both positives and negatives stemming from the increase of human mobility and tourism, therefore it is crucial to find a balance to encourage tourism for economic growth and stimulating sustainable incentives for the conservation of our oceans.

The ocean might seem endless, but we are all on the same boat and need to find mutual solutions to ride the waves together. This is crucial not only for our oceans and marine life, but for human survival.

26 March 2019

'Sustainable tourism' is not working – here's how we can change that

An article from The Conversation.

THE CONVERSATION

By Freya Higgins-Desbiolles, Senior Lecturer in Tourism, University of South Australia

This year is the United Nations' International Year of Sustainable Tourism for Development. UN World Tourism Organization Secretary-General Taleb Rifai declared it gave:

… a unique opportunity to advance the contribution of the tourism sector to the three pillars of sustainability – economic, social and environmental, while raising awareness of the true dimensions of a sector which is often undervalued.

Sustainable tourism comes from the concept of sustainable development, as set out in the 1987 Brundtland report. Sustainable development is:

… development which meets the needs of current generations without compromising the ability of future generations to meet their own needs.

British environmental activist George Monbiot argued that, over the years, sustainable development has morphed into sustained growth. The essence of his argument is that little resolve exists to go beyond rhetoric. This is because environmental crises require we limit the demands we place on it, but our economies require endless growth.

At the moment, economic growth trumps environmental limits, so sustainability remains elusive.

What is sustainable tourism?

Tourism is important to our efforts to achieve sustainable development. It is a massive industry, and many countries rely on it for their economies.

In 2016, more than 1.2 billion people travelled as tourists internationally, and another 6 billion people travelled domestically.

According to the UN World Tourism Organization, sustainable tourism is:

… tourism that takes full account of its current and future economic, social and environmental impacts, addressing the needs of visitors, the industry, the environment and host communities.

Following on from Monbiot's criticism, we might ask if efforts are directed at 'sustaining tourism', or instead harnessing tourism for wider sustainable development goals.

No place is off the tourism circuit

Looking at some of the tourism trouble spots, complacency is not called for.

Venice residents have accused tourists of 'destroying their city'. Barcelona's government has passed legislation to limit

new tourist accommodation. The Galapagos sees mass tourism's arrival threatening the iconic wildlife that attracts visitors.

No place is off the tourism circuit, so tourism grows with few limits. Ironically, tourists even want to tour Antarctica to see its pristine environment before it disappears ('last-chance tourism'). This is despite their impacts contributing to global warming and threatening this last wild place.

It is difficult to get a complete picture of the impacts of tourism because no-one is working to build a comprehensive view. So, insights are fragmented.

While we might be sceptical that UN 'years' are often more rhetoric than real, we can nonetheless seize the opportunity to make tourism more sustainable.

How can tourism be made more sustainable?

Tourism can be made more sustainable through several achievable measures. Some look to technological solutions so we can continue business as usual. Others highlight conscious consumerism and ideas like slow travel.

But in a world in which growing populations with endless consumer demands are pitted against a fragile environment, we require more concerted effort.

1. **Governments** must implement policies that foster sustainable development by overcoming the growth fetish. Tourism then should be developed only within sustainable development parameters. Governments must tackle the environmental limits to growth and climate change challenges we confront. Tourism development requires integrated planning. So, we need the government tourism authorities – such as Tourism Australia or state tourism commissions – focused equally on integrated planning as the marketing they currently emphasise.

2. **Consumers** should be educated for responsible travel choices. For example, few realise that all-inclusive resorts result in economic benefits from tourism leaking out of the host economy back to the home economies of the big multinationals and corporations that often own such resorts (think Club Med). Civics education in schools could educate for responsible travel.

3. **Local communities**, often treated as only one stakeholder among the many, must have a right to participate in tourism decision-making and have a say on If and how their communities become tourism destinations.

4. **Workers of tourism** must have their rights respected and given decent conditions. Tourism should not be allowed to continue as a low-wage and precarious source of employment.

5. **The tourism industry** needs to assume greater responsibility, submitting to local tax regimes and regulations so its presence builds thriving communities, rather than undermining them. This is increasingly essential as a social licence to operate. The industry should also educate its clients on responsible tourism.

6. **Non-governmental organisations** are essential for reporting on the abuses of tourism, including land grabs, human rights abuses, community opposition and corruption.

Harnessing these essential stakeholders in a rigorous agenda for sustainable development, rather than sustaining tourism, would make the UN's 'year' more meaningful.

19 April 2017

Five examples of sustainable tourism around the world

By Sarah Farell

Tourism is one of the fastest growing sectors in the world and can provide an essential economic boost for countries pitching themselves as holiday destinations. Tourism, however, has historically had devastating effects on the environment, people and their cultural identities.

Enter the concept of sustainable tourism, which according to the United Nations World Tourism Organization must:

◆ Conserve environmental resources and protect biodiversity

◆ Respect and preserve the cultures of host communities whilst benefiting them

◆ Address the needs of the visitors and industry whilst providing socio-economic benefit to all.

In order for tourism to continue and for us to live within our planetary bounds and respect all people, the only option is for the world to move away from unconscious, mass tourism and learn from the existing examples of thriving sustainable tourism models.

What are some examples of sustainable tourism?

1. Controlled tourism in Bhutan

Bhutan, located in the East of the Himalayas, is known as one of the happiest countries in the world. The country remains relatively untouched by colonialism which has ensured that the people's sustainable way of life has remained in tact.

Bhutan's tourism operates on the principle of 'high value, low impact'. This has been achieved by enforcing strict entry requirements and a daily visitor tariff. The daily tariff includes necessary expenses for the visit such as accommodation, a licensed tour guide, meals and hiking equipment. A large portion of the tariff, however, is used to maintain and develop the country's infrastructure, as well as contribute towards Bhutan's free health care and education.

2. A solar powered resort in Fiji

Six Senses Fiji, located on the tropical Malolo Island, is a five-star resort with sustainable luxury and cultural awareness at its core. The resort runs on 100% solar power, equipped with rainwater capture and its own onsite water-filtration site to eliminate the use of single-use plastic bottles. The resort aims to be as low-waste as possible, encouraging the principles of reuse whilst also practising recycling and composting with a 'worm-based septic system' and growing as much of its own herbs and vegetables as possible.

All handiwork and artwork at the hotel has been produced by local villagers and the hotel supports the Rise Beyond the Reef Charity which aims to bridge 'the divide between remote communities, government and the private sector in the South Pacific, sustainably creating a better world for women and children'.

3. A community run backpacker in South Africa

Mdumbi, a backpacker on the Wild Coast of South Africa, aims to promote 'community involvement and sustainable eco-tourism'. The backpacker prides itself in being fused with the amaXhosa culture of the Eastern Cape, situated deep in the heart of a traditional village.

WIth a number of sustainability interventions onsite such as energy efficiency, solar power and waste management, Mdumbi has a unique ownership model, with the local employees, the amaXhosa community association, and TransCape (Mdumbi's affiliated NPO) all holding shares in the business.

Mdumbi's NPO, TransCape, aims 'to provide access to the resources, support, and knowledge necessary for communities to initiate the process of change towards a better quality of life'. In 2017, the Backpacker was also awarded a silver prize by the World Responsible Tourism Awards for best in poverty reduction.

4. Conservation 'Voluntouring' in Belize

Responsible Travel, a responsible tourism operator based in the UK, advocates for more responsible travel decisions through online content and organising sustainable and ethical holiday packages. One such package offers individuals the opportunity to volunteer at a conservation organisation in Belize.

Tourists are offered the opportunity to 'join a team of local conservationists and experts as part of a volunteer group working five days a week in the rainforests of Belize'. Volunteers are strictly vetted and provided with a volunteer guide before departing, as well as caller support in order to ensure that the voluntourism is done ethically and respectfully to locals, animals and the environment. Some of their guidelines are illustrated in their infographic above.

5. A sustainable tour operator come foundation in Switzerland

The Swiss Foundation for Solidarity in Tourism (SST) is a non-profit foundation that grew out of one of the leading tour operators in Switzerland. The foundation, founded in 2001, supports projects and organisations in Switzerland and worldwide which look to improve the livelihoods of people in tourist destinations, contribute to sustainable tourism development and contribute to 'intercultural understandings' between travellers and locals.

By providing grants to deserving projects, the foundation hopes to further develop sustainable tourism online and on the ground.

These are but a few of many varying examples of models for sustainable tourism development. As the world moves towards sustainability in every facet and every industry, there is no doubt that the tourism industry will need an unprecedented overhaul in order to move towards low-impact and meaningful travel experiences that do not detriment people or the world on which we rely.

12 April 2019

Key Facts

- There were 71.7 million visits overseas by UK residents in 2018, a decrease of 1% compared with 2017. (page 2)

- UK residents spent £45.4 billion on visits abroad in 2018, which was 1% more than in 2017. (page 3)

- Overseas residents spent £22.9 billion on visits to the UK in 2018, a decrease of 7% compared with 2017. (page 3)

- There were 3.9 million visits to the UK by residents of the USA in 2018, more than any other country. (page 3)

- London attracted 19.1 million overnight visits in 2018, far more than any other town or city. (page 4)

- There were 47.0 million holiday visits abroad by UK residents, 1% more than in 2017 and accounting for almost two-thirds (66%) of visits. (page 4)

- There were 15.6 million visits to Spain by UK residents in 2018, a decrease of 2% from 2017 and the first time this number has fallen since 2009. (page 5)

- In 2018, there were a record 1.4 billion international tourist arrivals, according to the World Tourism Organization (UNWTO), a rise of 6% over 2017. (page 6)

- In 1950, there were 25 million international tourist visits, rising to 166 million in 1970, and 435 million in 1990. (page 6)

- Europe leads the way in overseas visits, receiving 713 million visitors last year alone. (page 6)

- In 2017, Chinese tourists made 143 million journeys abroad. (page 6)

- The tourist industry is responsible for about 2.5% of British GDP. (page 7)

- Thomas Cook, one of the world's biggest leisure travel groups, with sales of £7.8 billion, 19 million annual customers and 22,000 employees, ceased trading in September 2019. (page 10)

- In 2016, UK residents went on more than 45 million foreign holidays, up from 27 million in 1996. (page 11)

- Between 1996 and 2015 (the most recent figures available from the Civil Aviation Authority), passenger numbers at UK airports increased by 85%, from 135 million to 251 million. (page 12)

- The number of holidaymakers travelling by sea has declined by 33% since 1996. (page 12)

- More than half of us (57%) hold an unfavourable opinion of British tourists, and just 29% take a positive view. (page 14)

- More than six in ten (61%) think that residents have a negative opinion of British tourists, and only 23% believe that we are gladly received by natives. (page 14)

- Filipinos are the most likely to think their tourists are greeted with a smile (83%). (page 15)

- There was a slight decrease in the numbers of British people arrested abroad in 2013/14. (page 15)

- Tourism accounts for 10% of the world's GDP. (page 18)

- Tourism contributed $8.8 trillion to the world economy in 2018, with 319 million people employed in the industry (page 23)

- 1% of English residents are responsible for nearly a fifth of all flights abroad. (page 24)

- The 10% most frequent flyers in England took more than half of all international flights in 2018. (page 24)

- 48% of the population did not take a single flight abroad in 2018. (page 24)

- Two-thirds of people (67%) felt that we should limit air travel in order to address climate change. (page 26)

- The tourism industry's carbon footprint around the planet grew by 15% from 3.9 to 4.5 gigatons of equivalent carbon dioxide. (page 27)

- Tourism accounts for 8% of the world's carbon emissions. (page 29)

- Tourists now account for nearly 60% of air travel. (page 30)

- Cruise ships in the Caribbean produce over 70,000 tons of waste annually. (page 30)

- Tourists cause a 40 per cent surge in waste entering the Mediterranean Sea, 95 per cent of which is plastic. (page 32)

- While the Mediterranean holds only 1 per cent of the world's water, it contains 7 per cent of all of the world's microplastic waste. (page 32)

- Scientists are predicting that 90% of the world's coral reefs will die by 2050. (page 34)

- The number of international tourist trips worldwide reached 1.3 billion in 2017, and is predicted to reach 1.8 billion by 2030. (page 34)

- 14,000 tonnes of toxic sunscreen make their way to the underwater world each year. (page 35)

- Researchers estimate that an additional 8 million metric tonnes of plastic ends up in the ocean every year. (page 35)

- In 2016, more than 1.2 billion people travelled as tourists internationally, and another 6 billion people travelled domestically. (page 36)

Glossary

Alternative tourism

Any form of tourism that differs from the 'mass market': for example, tornado chasing, couch surfing or visiting sites of natural disasters, as opposed to beach or package holidays.

Conservation

Safeguarding biodiversity; attempting to protect endangered species and their habitats from destruction.

Dark tourism

Tourism that involves travelling to places associated with death and suffering.

Domestic tourism

Residents holidaying within their own country, for example Britons who holiday in Cornwall.

Eco-friendly

Policies, procedures, laws, goods or services that have a minimal or reduced impact on the environment.

Ecotourism

Ecotourism is closely related to 'responsible tourism' and generally refers to a form of travel that is conscious of preserving both the ecology and the local culture/community of a tourist destination.

Green tourism

The concept of green tourism is very similar to 'ecotourism'. Green tourism involves thinking about how you reach your destination (for example, taking public transport instead of driving) as well as the impact you have on the local environment once you arrive.

Overtourism

When a destination attracts too many tourists, and so a negative effect is had on the local residents and environment.

Philanthropy

The concept of helping other human beings in an outward-looking, altruistic way, usually in the form of a charitable donation of money or property towards an institution that would benefit from help.

Poverty tourism

Poverty tourism refers to the practice of visiting extremely poor areas or communities in search of an 'authentic' experience. Poverty tourism often involves 'slum tours', in which tourists are led around sites such as the favelas of Rio di Janeiro or taken to visit the street children of Delhi.

Responsible tourism

Responsible tourism has minimal social and environmental impacts. It is also beneficial to local communities.

Selfie

The selfie has become a huge part of modern life. A selfie is a photograph that a person takes of themselves, usually with a smartphone or digital camera, usually with the intent of sharing it on social media. It has transformed the simple self-portrait into something more immediate and has grown in cultural importance – it's been linked to identity, self-exploration and narcissism.

Staycation

A home-based holiday in which people stay in the country where they live.

Sustainability

Sustainability means living within the limits of the planet's resources to meet humanity's present-day needs without compromising those of future generations. Sustainable living should maintain a balanced and healthy environment.

Sustainable tourism

Sustainable tourism is closely linked to ecotourism and involves having as little impact as possible on local ecosystems and communities when visiting a destination. Sustainable tourists may choose to travel by rail instead of air, for example, and support local businesses instead of international companies.

Tourism

Tourism is the business of providing services, such as transportation, places to stay, or entertainment, for tourists.

Tourist

A person who is travelling away from home for the purpose of pleasure, such as someone going on holiday.

Voluntourism

Tourism which includes volunteer work as part of the tour or holiday experience. This is becoming increasingly popular, especially with gap year travellers. Examples include teaching English to children or carrying out environmental projects.

Wildlife

A collective term for wild animals and plants that grow and live independently of human beings.

Zero waste

A plan to promote the idea of recycling and re-using materials rather than just disposing of them. The aim is to reduce the amount of waste sent to landfills.

Activities

Brainstorming

- In small groups, brainstorm what you know about tourism:
  - What is tourism?
  - What different types of tourism are there?
  - Why do tourists visit the UK?
  - Why do people go abroad?
- In pairs, list ways that you can be a 'responsible tourist'.
- In small groups, make a list of the different reasons that people may have for travel.
- In pairs, list different jobs that are related to the tourism industry.

Research

- Conduct a survey amongst your classmates to find out what kind of holidays people go on. You should ask at least five questions and write a report summarising your results. You should also include graphs.
- Choose a destination and research eco-friendly accommodation options. Write down as many options as you can find and feedback to your class.
- Domestic tourism is becoming more popular in the UK, with increasing numbers of Britons choosing to holiday in their own country rather than abroad. Think about places close to you and why they might be good locations for a holiday. Look into details of local accommodation, activities and interesting sights, then design a tourist brochure based on your findings.
- Research a tourist destination of your choice and evaluate the positive and negative effects of tourism on that location. How can tourism to this area be made more responsible and sustainable?

Design

- Choose one of the articles from this topic and create your own illustration to accompany it.
- Create a travel brochure for your local town that will include suggestions of activities, places to visit and accommodation options.
- Design a poster that will encourage people to take a staycation.
- Imagine you work for a charity that promotes green travel. Design a campaign to raise awareness amongst young adults. Your campaign could include posters, TV adverts, radio adverts, social media marketing or website banners. Work in small groups.
- In pairs, choose a holiday destination. You should each research how much a four-night trip to your chosen destination would cost for two adults. However, one of you should make your holiday 'green' and the other 'mainstream'. Make sure you report a breakdown of costs: for example, accommodation and flights. Compare your findings with your partner's. Is 'green' travel more expensive?

Oral

- Create a PowerPoint presentation that will inform your school about what it means to be a responsible tourist.
- In pairs, discuss the positive and negative effects tourism can have on a community or destination. Write down your ideas and share with the rest of your class.
- Imagine you have a friend or relative who has never been abroad, how would you persuade them to try visiting another country? Role play the exchange in pairs.
- In small groups, discuss whether overtourism is a problem or not.

Reading/writing

- Write a definition of the term 'overtourism'.
- What is responsible tourism? Write 500 words exploring this question.
- What do you think holidays will look like in 100 years time? Write a blog post exploring this question.
- Choose one of the articles and write a short summary. Pick out five key points from the article and list them.
- Imagine you are a resident in one of the areas that has an overtourism problem. Write a diary entry of the problems the tourists cause in your area.
- Read *Why there's nothing wrong with being a tourist*. Do you agree with the opinions in the article? If not, then why? Write your reasons down.
- Choose two articles in this book that have opposing or different views. Compare and contrast the articles and write a short essay on your findings.
- Read *Global tourism leaves a giant carbon footprint*, and write a blogpost on how you can travel in the most carbon-friendly ways.

Acknowledgements

The publisher is grateful for permission to reproduce the material in this book. While every care has been taken to trace and acknowledge copyright, the publisher tenders its apology for any accidental infringement or where copyright has proved untraceable. The publisher would be pleased to come to a suitable arrangement in any such case with the rightful owner.

Images

Cover image courtesy of iStock. All other images courtesy of Pixabay and Unsplash, except page 7 & 15; Rawpixel

Icons

Icons on pages 17, 33 & 39 were made by freepik from www. freepik.com.

Illustrations

Don Hatcher: pages 13 & 35. Simon Kneebone: pages 31 & 38. Angelo Madrid: pages 5 & 28.

Additional acknowledgements

With thanks to the Independence team: Shelley Baldry, Danielle Lobban, Jackie Staines and Jan Sunderland.

Tracy Biram

Cambridge, January 2020